"Bless the Black-Footed Ferrets for hanging on with their fierce and graceful hold on life. Bless the Prairie Dogs and the power of their predator-prey dance with Black-Footed Ferrets—that is an invitation for a myriad of other animals to live with them. And bless Elaine Miller Bond for not only caring about these endangered species, but inspiring us to care, too. By offering a glimpse into their extraordinary lives, we recognize a world without Black-Footed Ferrets and Prairie Dogs is an incomplete world. Long live the Endangered Species Act that protects these precious wild lives that are threatened."

—Terry Tempest Williams
Author of *Finding Beauty in a Broken World*

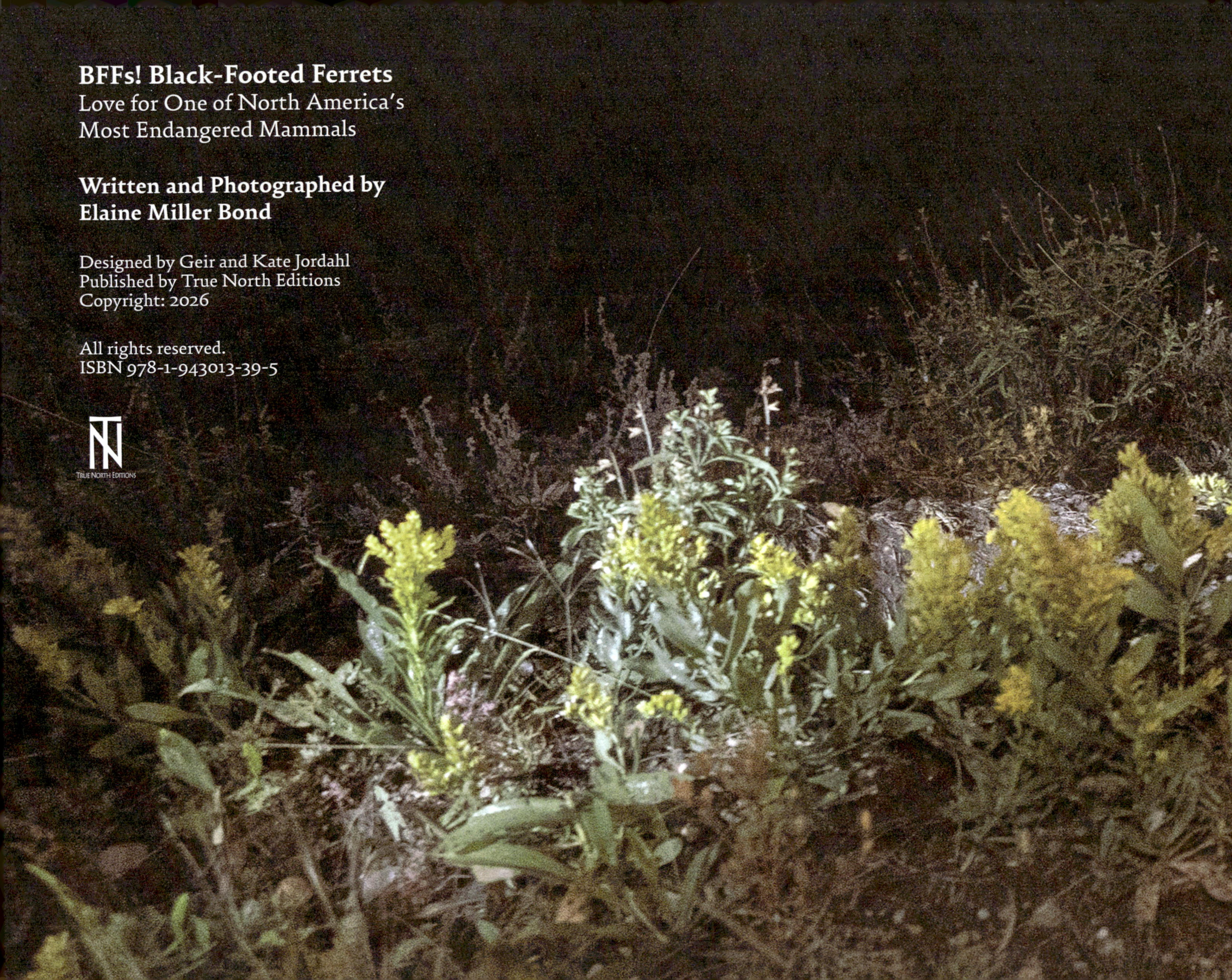

BFFs! Black-Footed Ferrets
Love for One of North America's
Most Endangered Mammals

**Written and Photographed by
Elaine Miller Bond**

Designed by Geir and Kate Jordahl
Published by True North Editions
Copyright: 2026

ISBN 978-1-943013-39-5

True North Editions

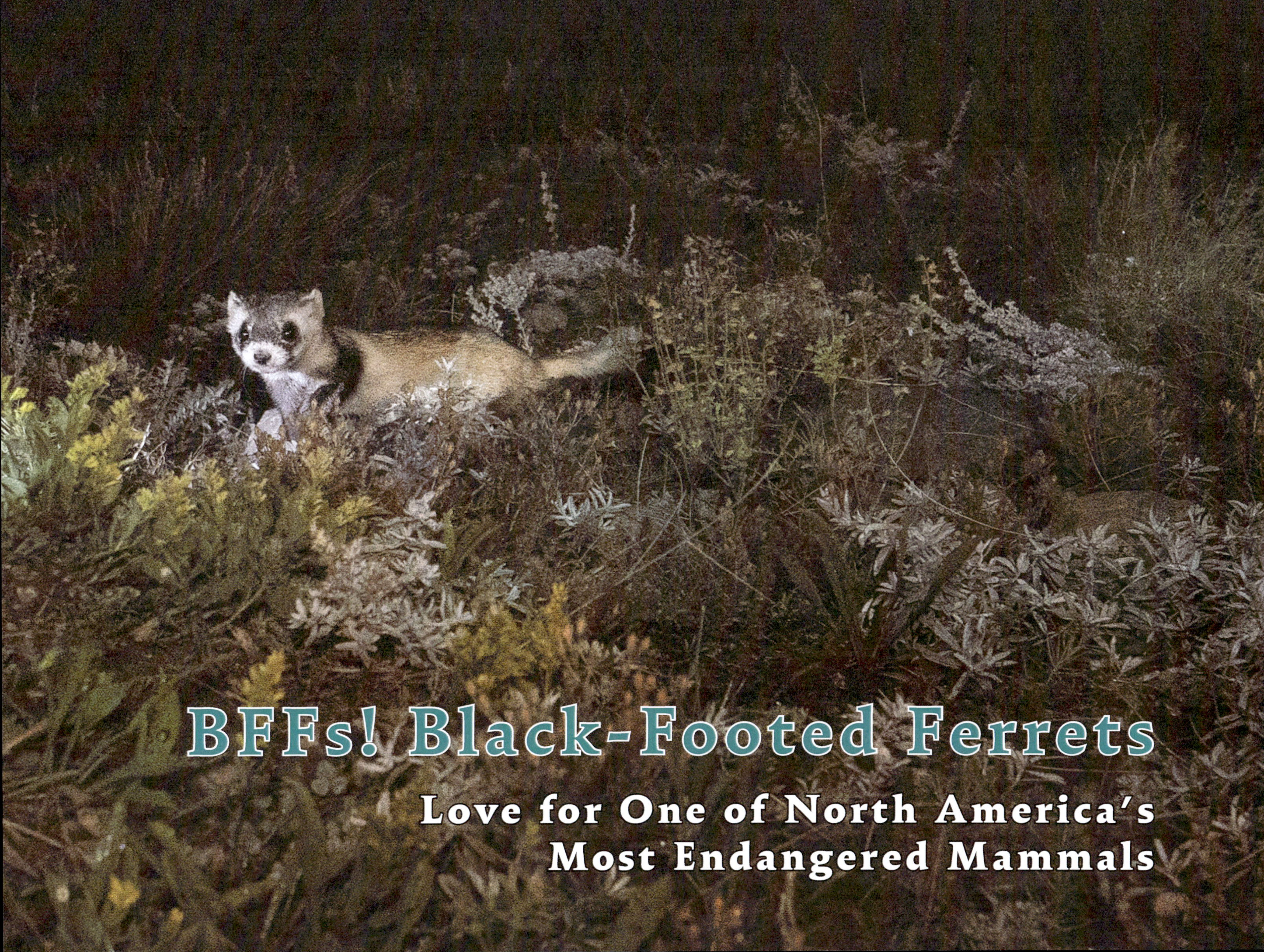

BFFs! Black-Footed Ferrets
Love for One of North America's
Most Endangered Mammals

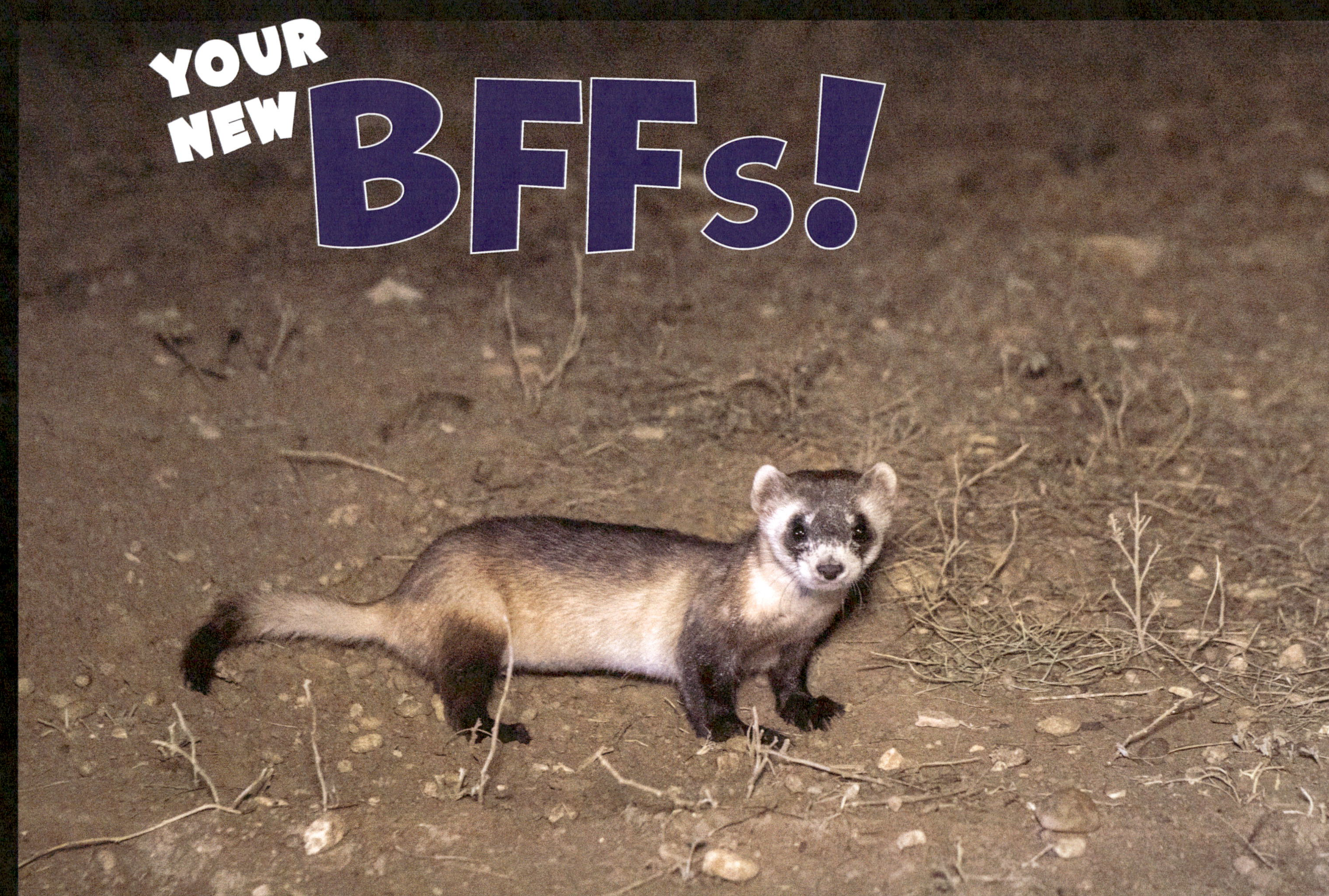

Black-Footed Ferrets are
YOUR
NEW
BFFs!

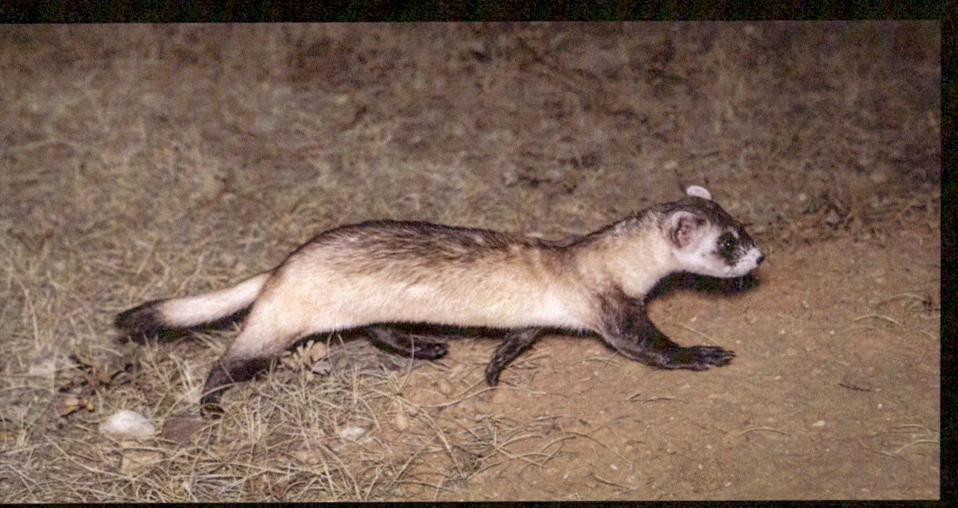 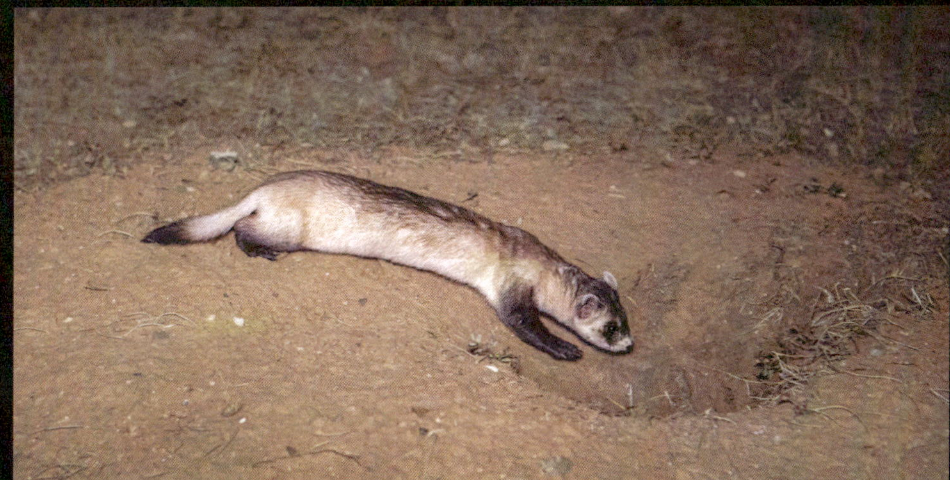

Meet the Black-Footed Ferret (BFF)—one of the most endangered mammals in North America . . . and also one of the most curious, playful, and adorable!

Once, up to half a million black-footed ferrets lived on the American prairies. Today, fewer than four hundred survive in the wild. BFFs are very rare. But that's not the only reason why most people never see them.

Black-footed ferrets lead secret lives.

BFFs ARE
night-loving and hidden.

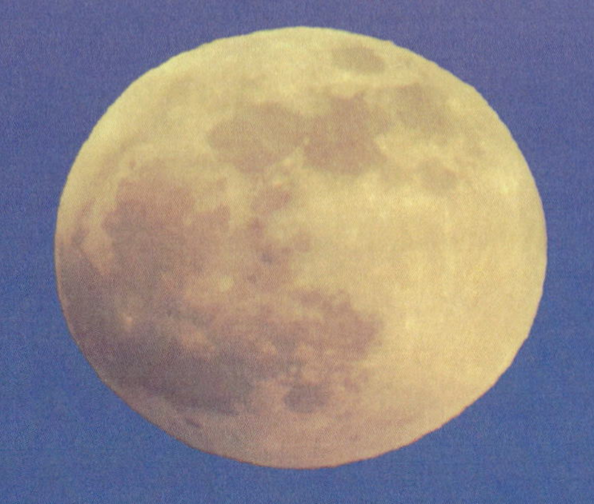

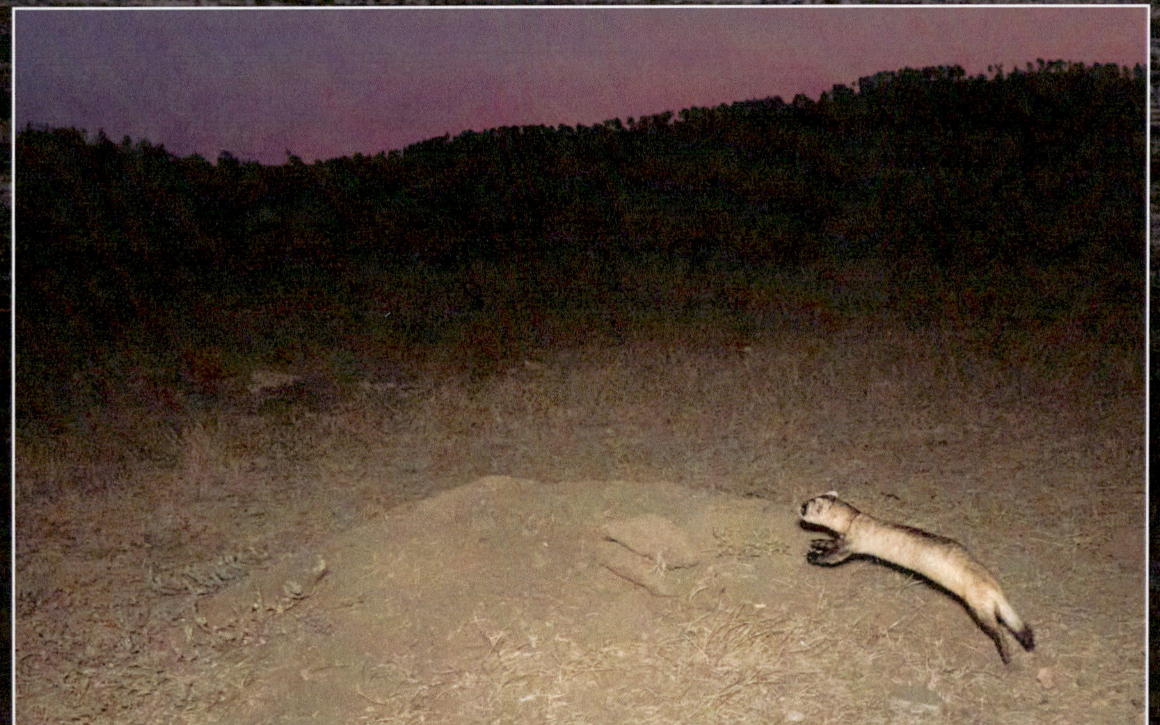

Black-footed ferrets live underground in prairie dog tunnels, known as burrows. Usually, they only come out at night.

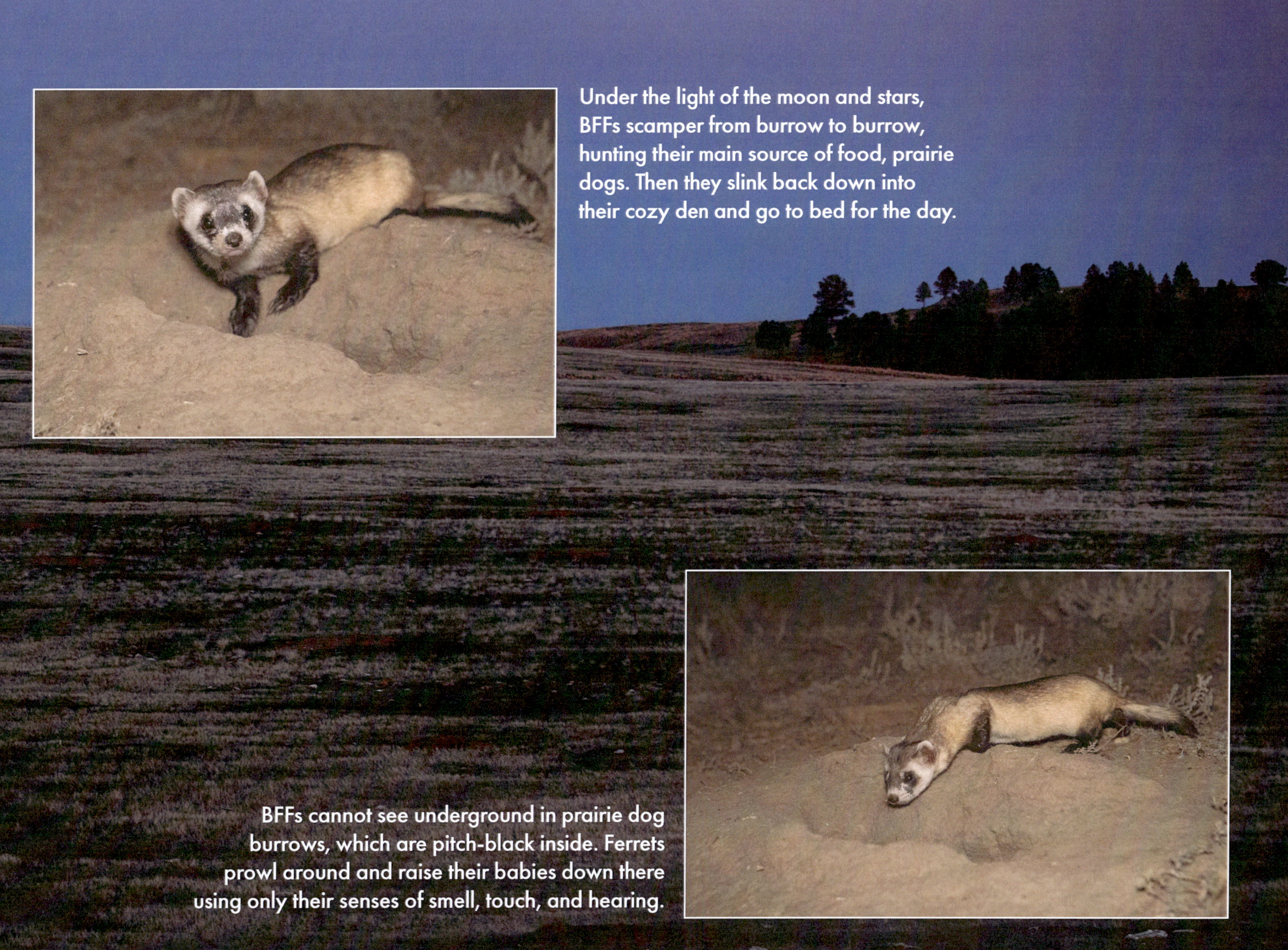

Under the light of the moon and stars, BFFs scamper from burrow to burrow, hunting their main source of food, prairie dogs. Then they slink back down into their cozy den and go to bed for the day.

BFFs cannot see underground in prairie dog burrows, which are pitch-black inside. Ferrets prowl around and raise their babies down there using only their senses of smell, touch, and hearing.

Black-footed ferret in a prairie dog hole.

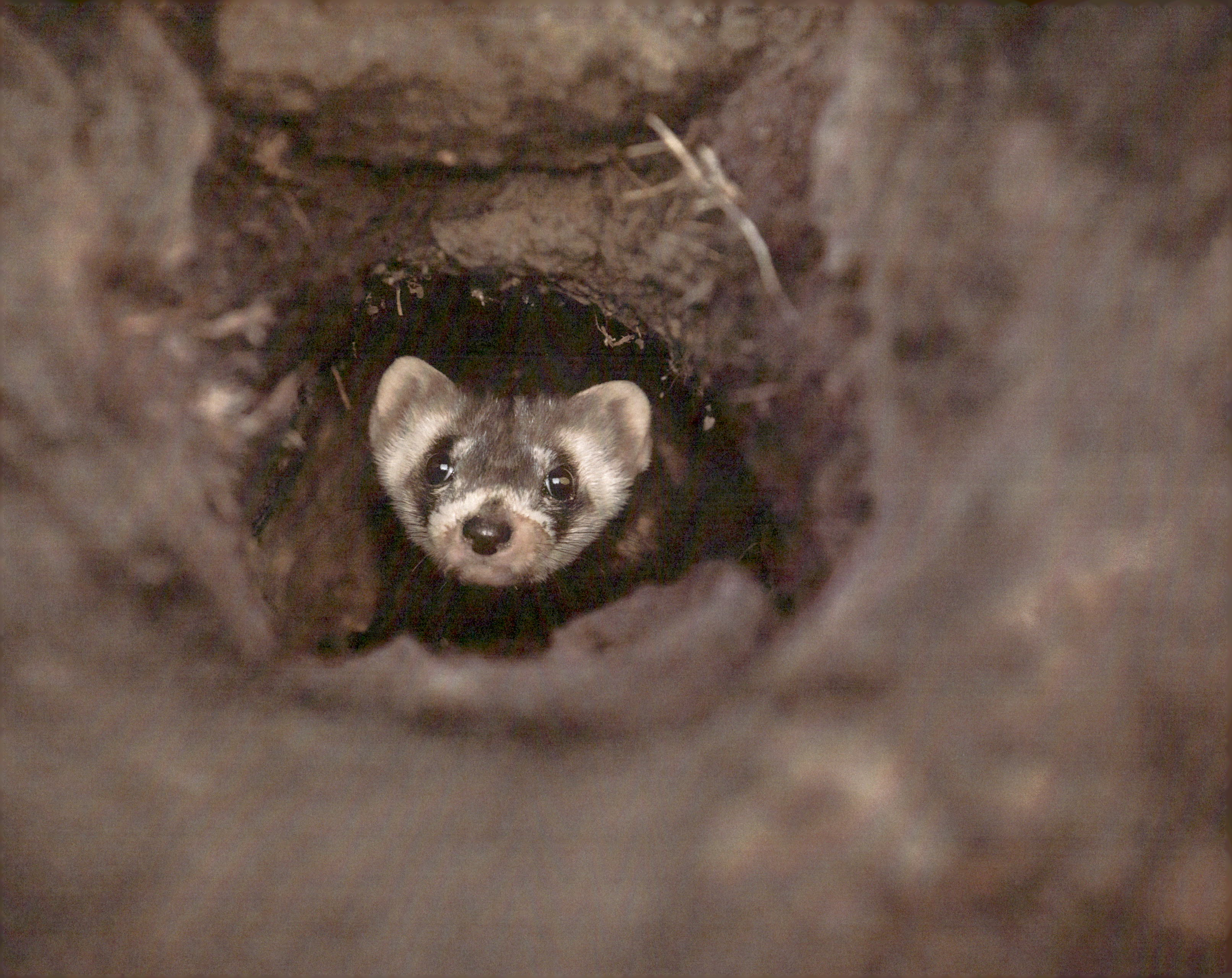

BFFs ARE
cuddly with their families.

Black-footed ferrets are territorial and live alone for most of their lives. If two or more BFFs are seen together, they are usually a mother and babies, called kits. Family members often touch noses or gently nibble one another to check in and show affection.

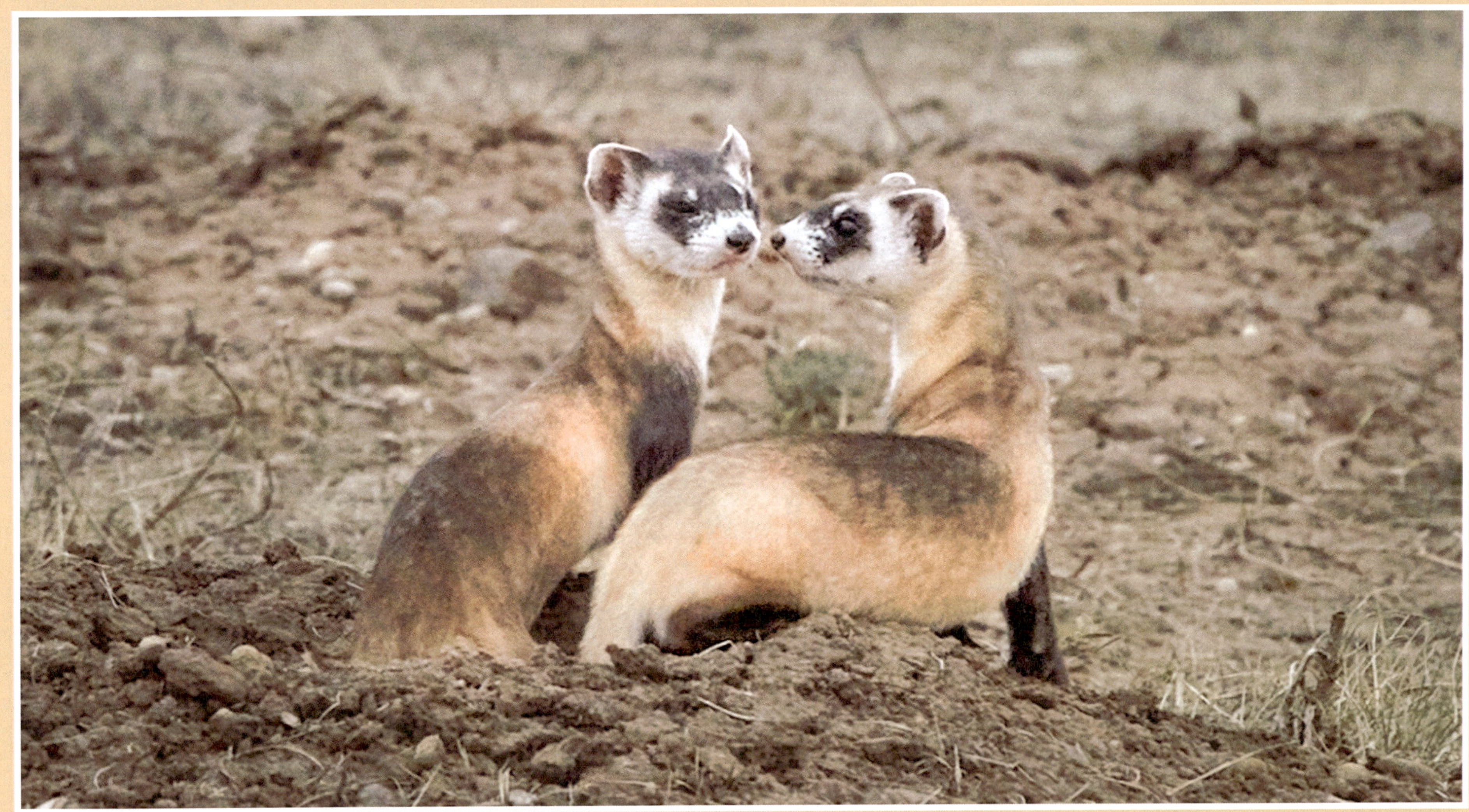

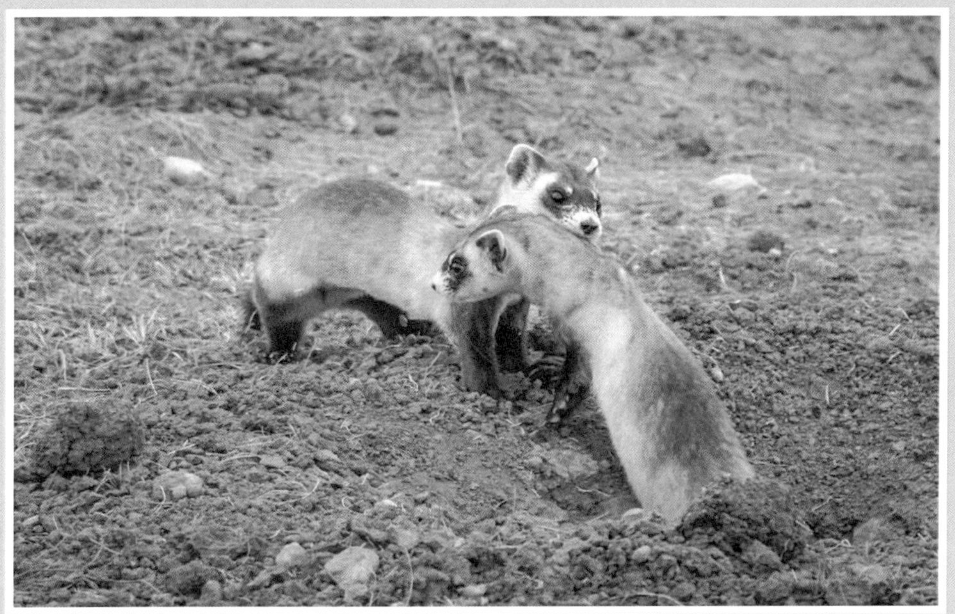

A mother carries a kit to a new den.

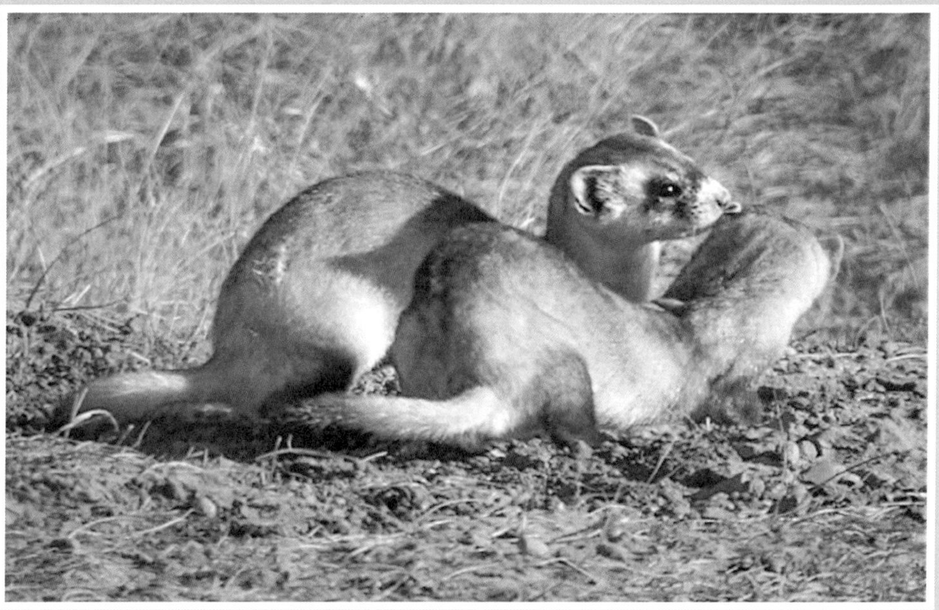

Gentle nibbles.

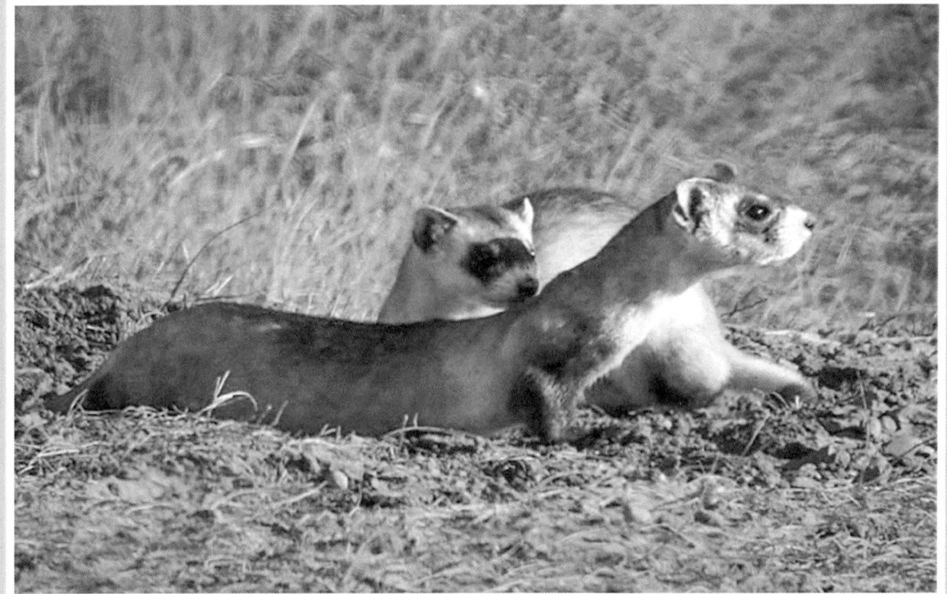

It is a special treat to see BFFs at dawn or dusk.

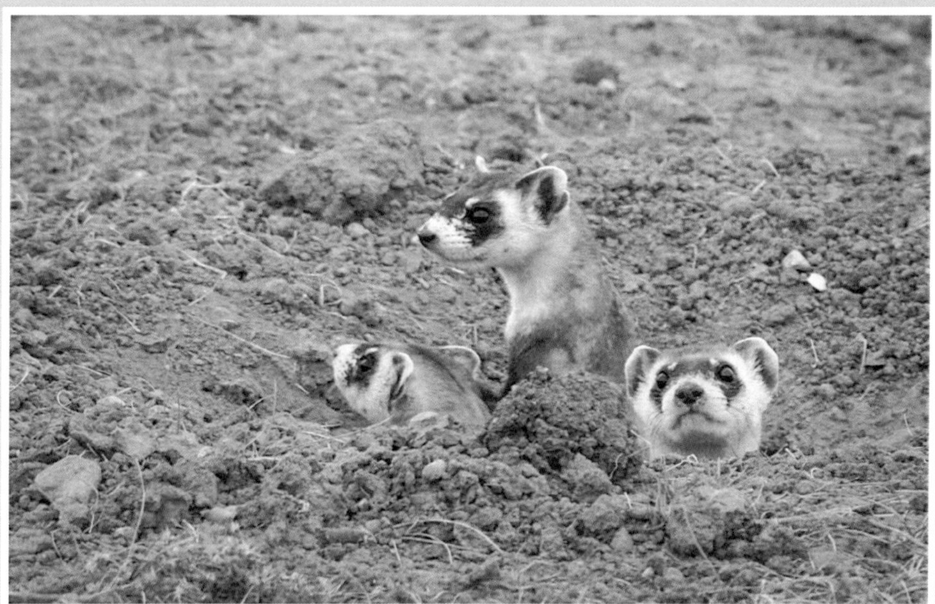

A mother, facing forward, with her kits.

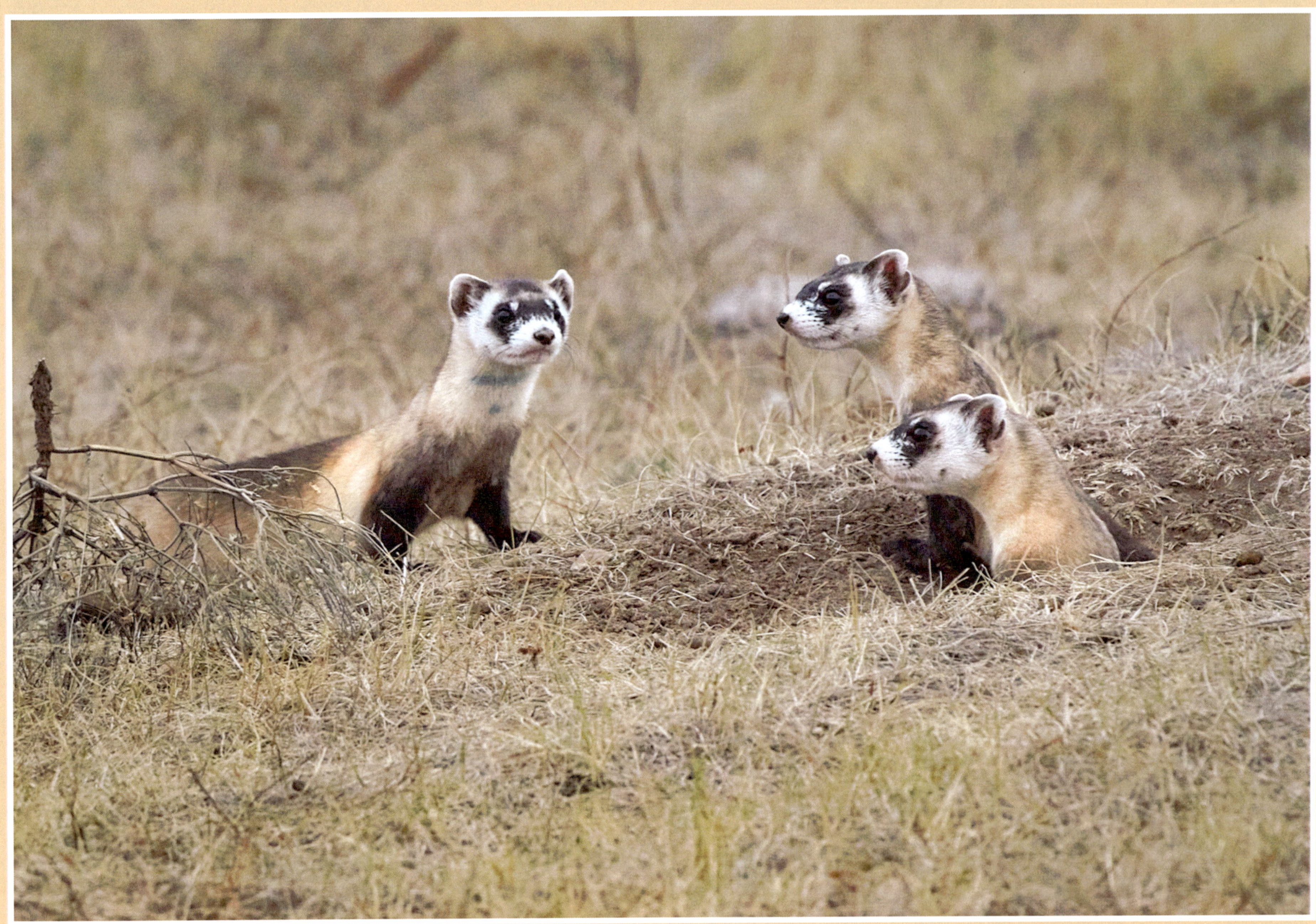

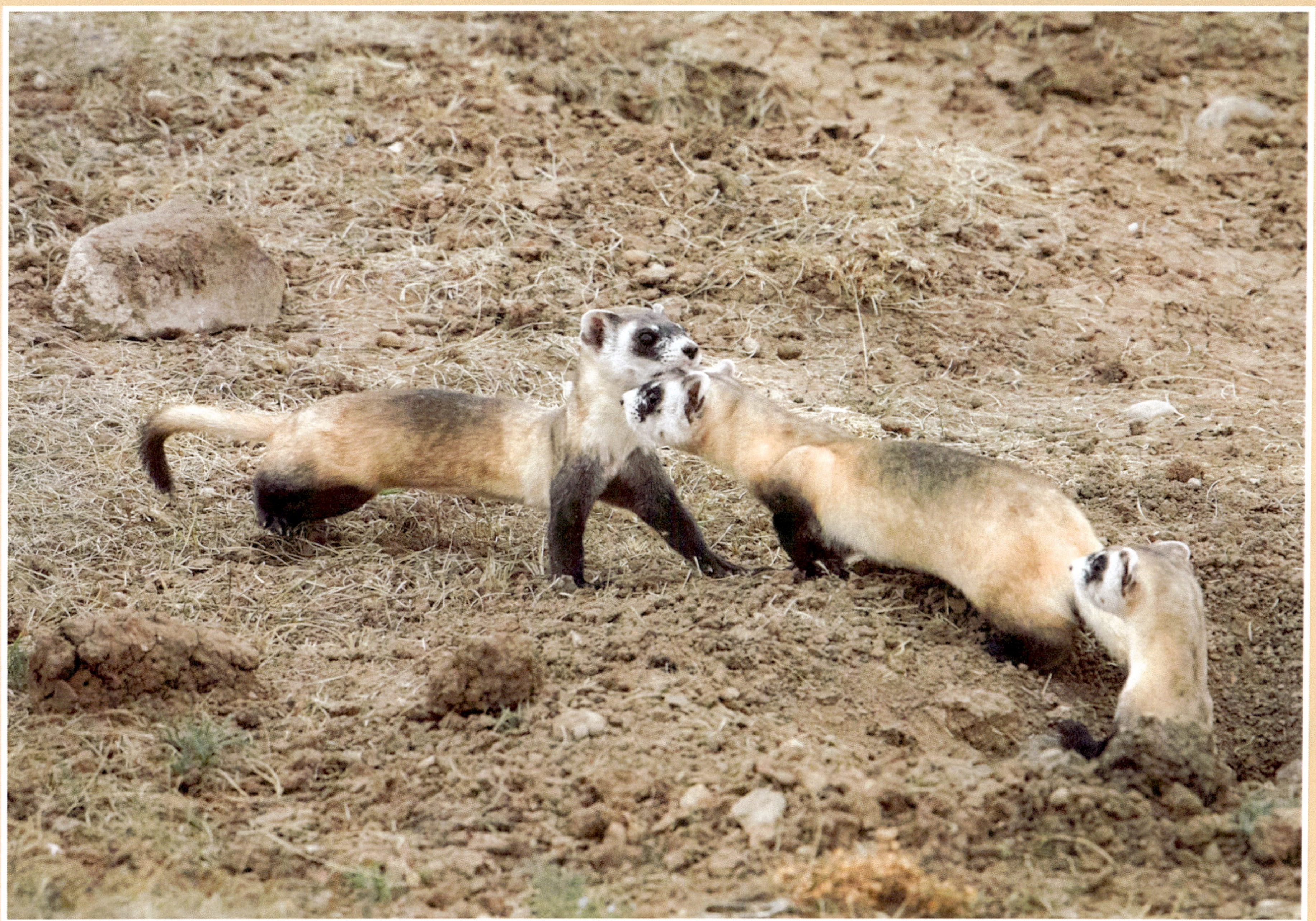

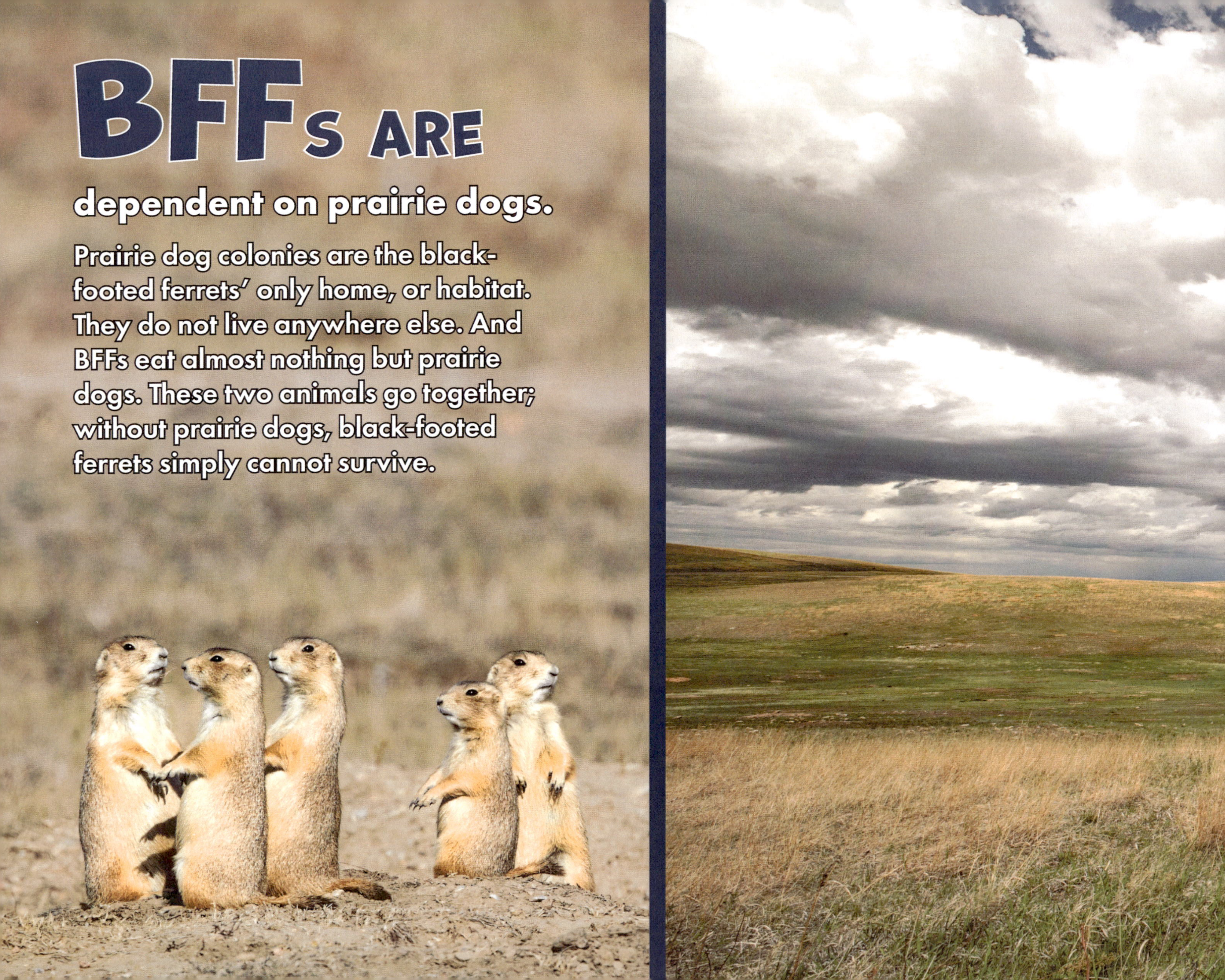

BFFs ARE

dependent on prairie dogs.

Prairie dog colonies are the black-footed ferrets' only home, or habitat. They do not live anywhere else. And BFFs eat almost nothing but prairie dogs. These two animals go together; without prairie dogs, black-footed ferrets simply cannot survive.

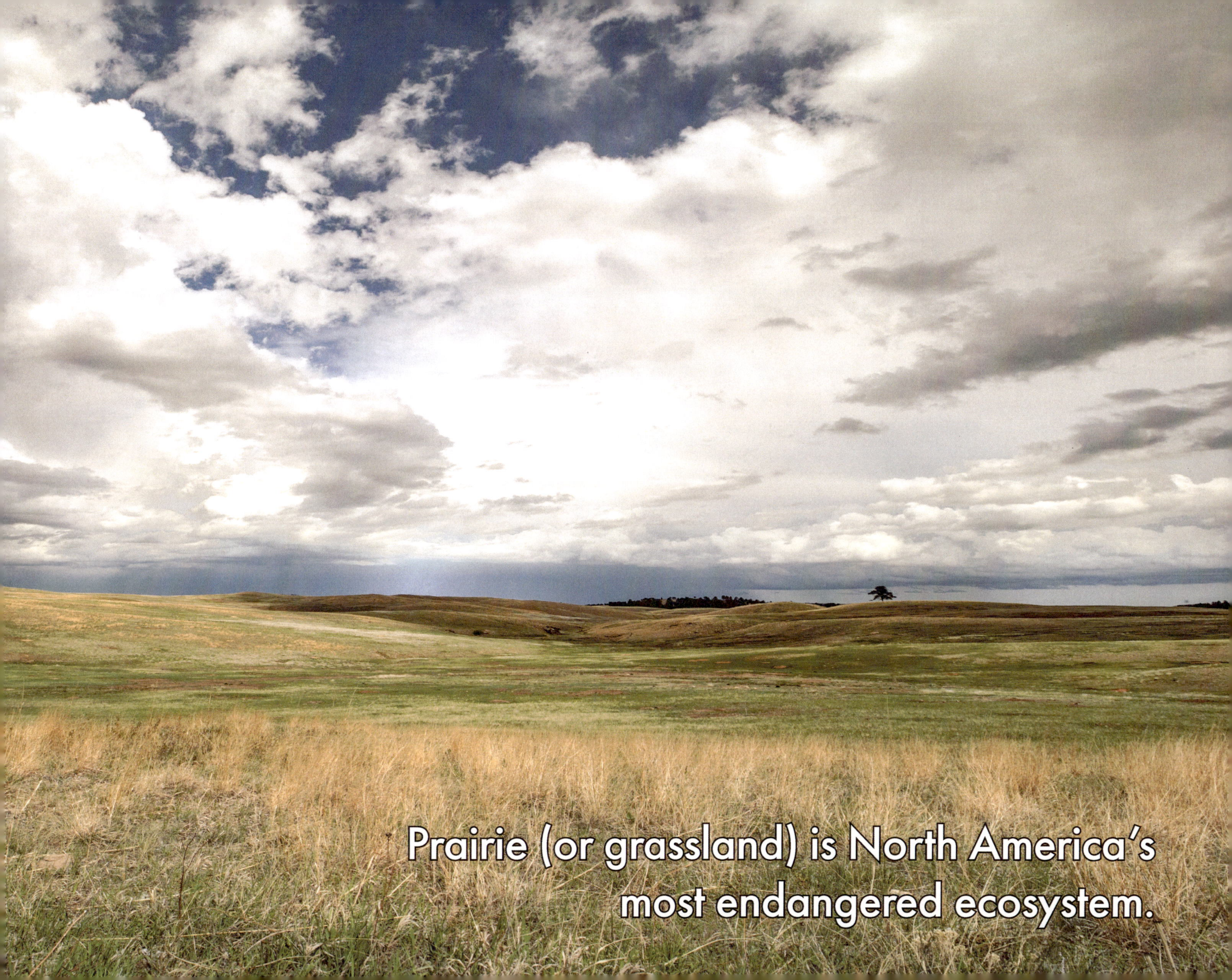
Prairie (or grassland) is North America's
most endangered ecosystem.

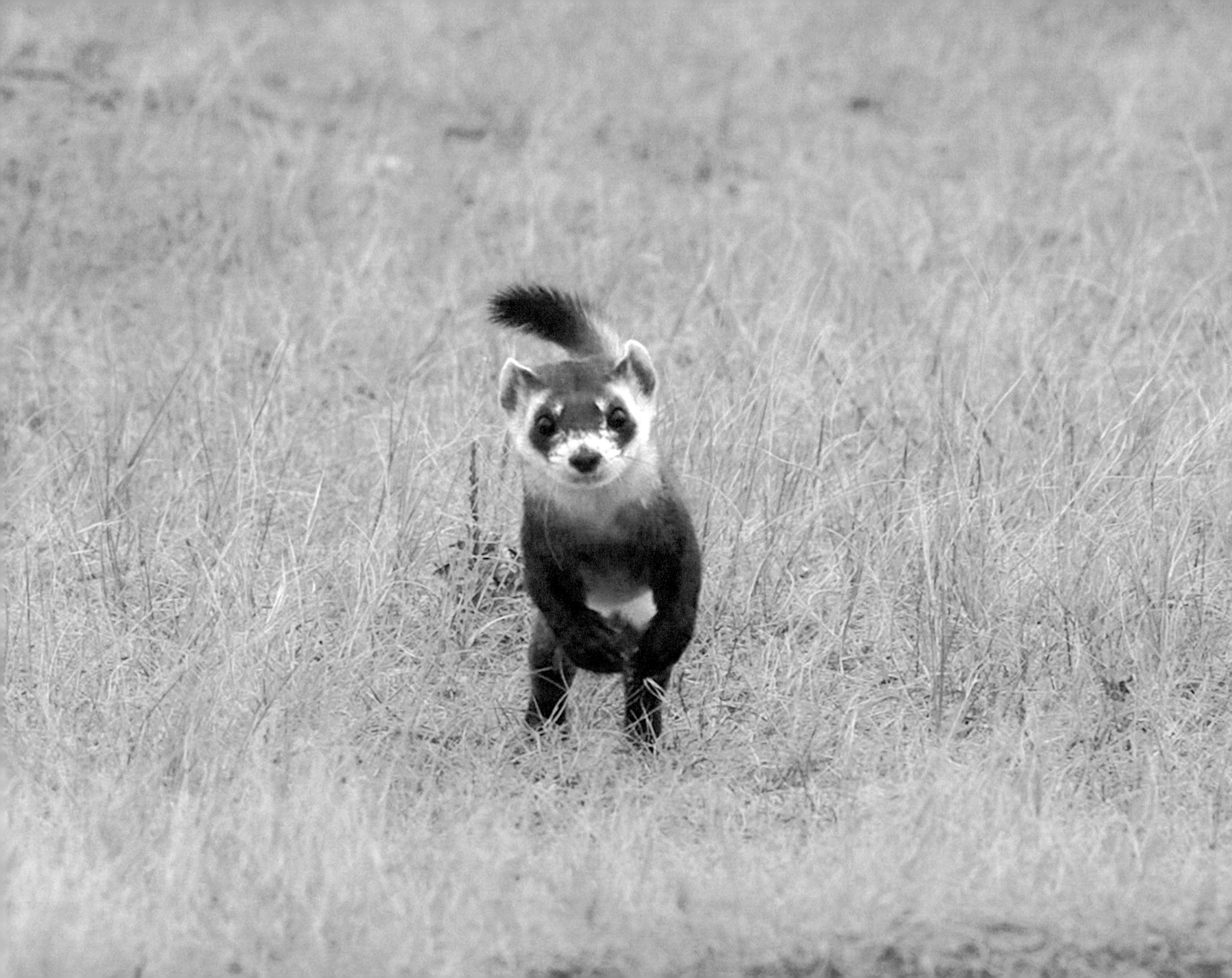

FERRET FOOD FACTS:

Can you eat a cheeseburger that's as big as you? BFFs must eat their own body weight in the form of prairie dogs every three days—more than one hundred prairie dogs in a year!

BFFs never waste food. They eat the entire prairie dog: fur, bones, and all!

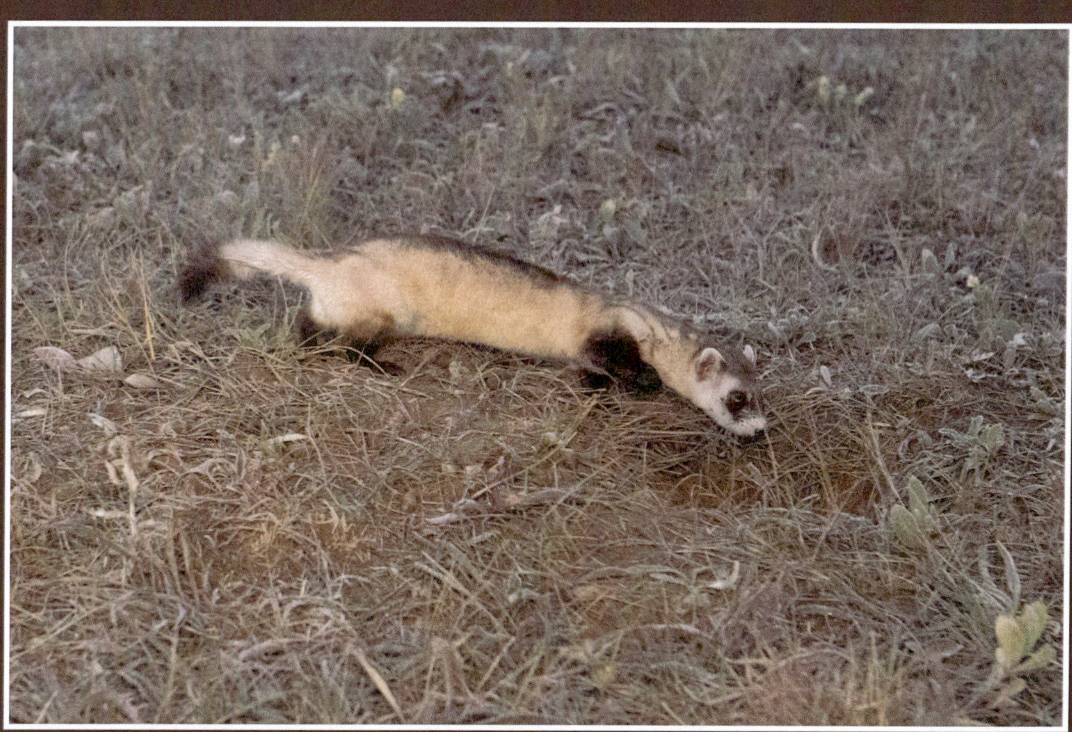

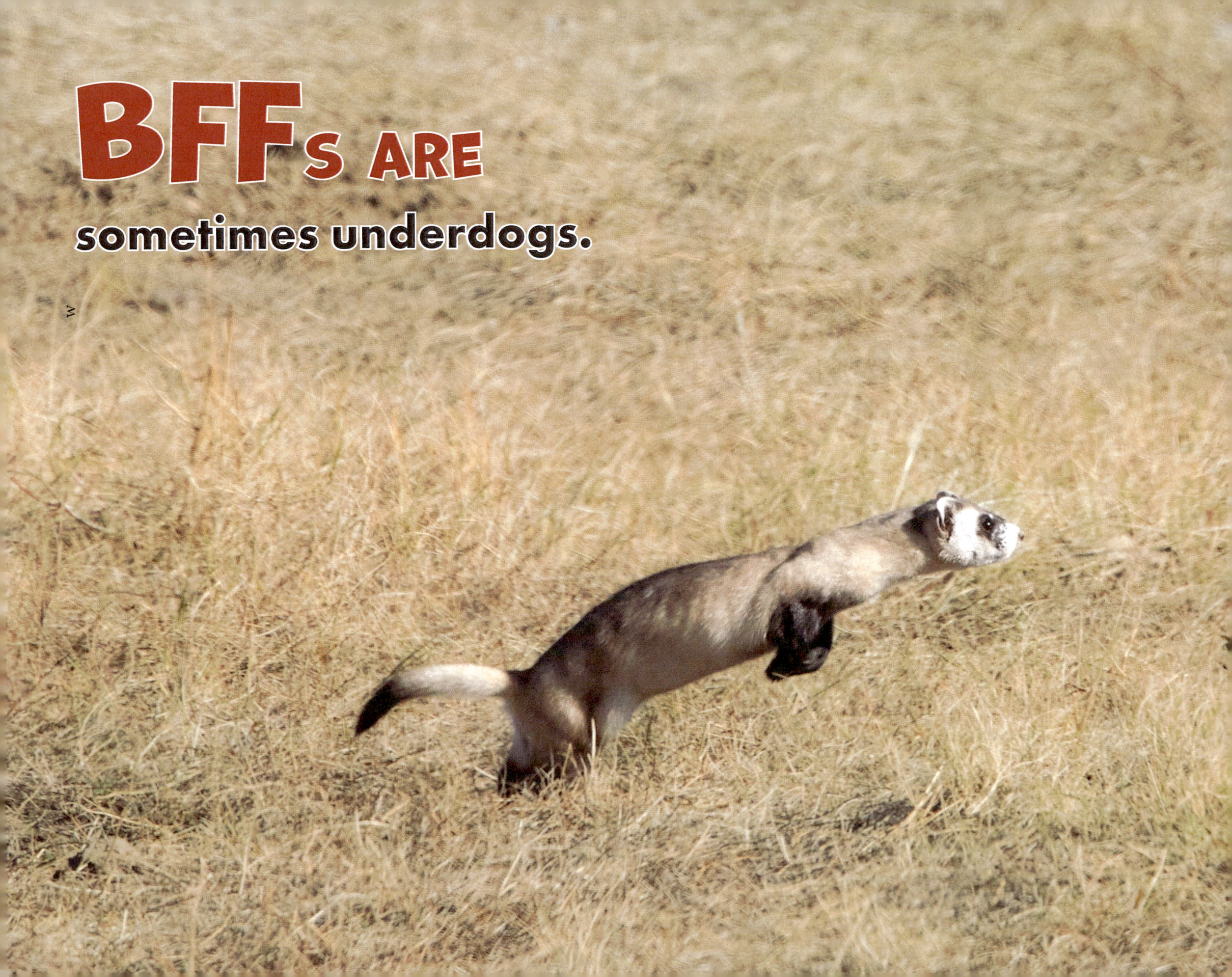

BFFs ARE
sometimes underdogs.

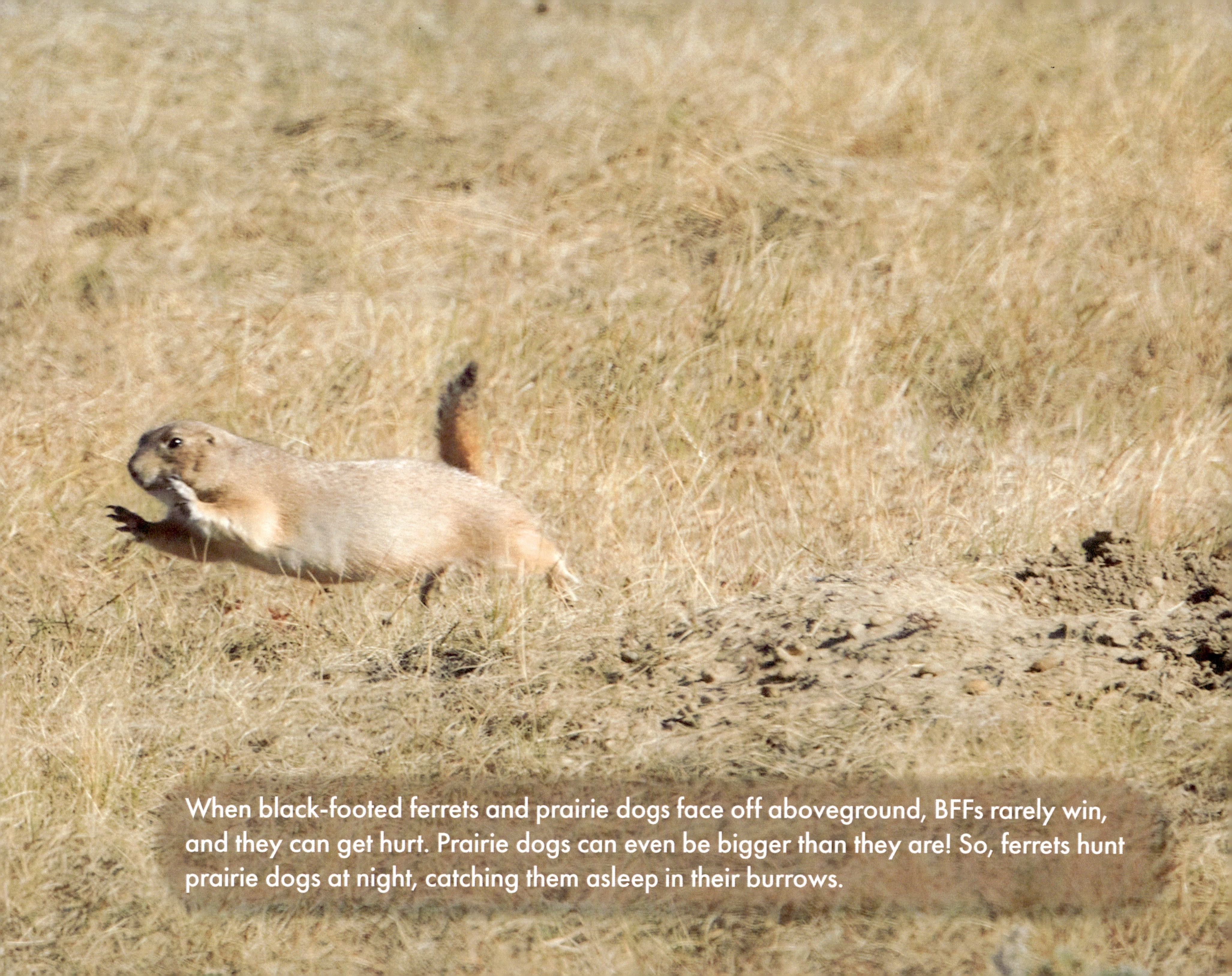

When black-footed ferrets and prairie dogs face off aboveground, BFFs rarely win, and they can get hurt. Prairie dogs can even be bigger than they are! So, ferrets hunt prairie dogs at night, catching them asleep in their burrows.

BFFs ARE

the only native ferrets of the Americas.

Black-footed ferrets belong to the weasel family, *Mustelidae*, along with otters, badgers, wolverines, minks, and more. Pet ferrets are a different species.

. . . slinky and stinky.

Scent glands help ferrets send messages, some of which smell skunky. BFFs rarely fight with each other. Scent-marking their territories might help them keep the peace!

. . . little, long, and super strong.

Black-footed ferrets only weigh between one and a half and two and a half pounds—about the weight of an eight-week-old kitten. But they can run carrying a prairie dog as heavy as they are!

1. Far-apart eyes help BFFs watch for danger all around.

2. Small mouselike ears.

3. A skinny body with no body fat means BFFs must eat a lot just to stay warm and active. And they need prairie dog holes to protect them from the cold and wet.

4. Scent glands are under the base of the tail and throughout the skin.

5. Short fur stays clean in dirt tunnels.

6. Short legs keep BFFs low to the ground, where they can pick up important scents.

7. Black feet!

8. Long whiskers and long hairs on the bottom of the paws help BFFs feel their way in total darkness.

9. A wide jaw with strong muscles helps them hunt and eat.

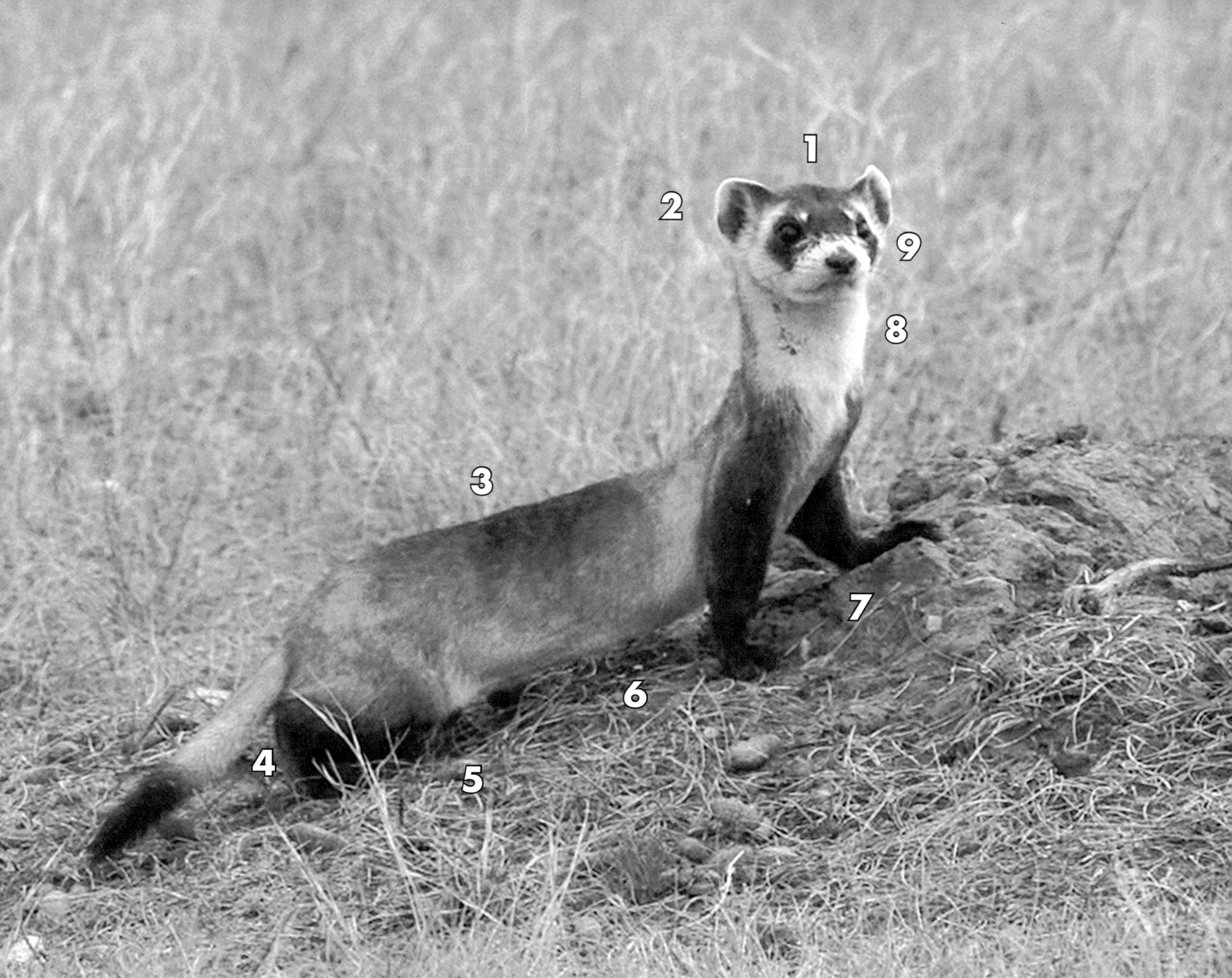

1
2
9
8
3
7
6
4
5

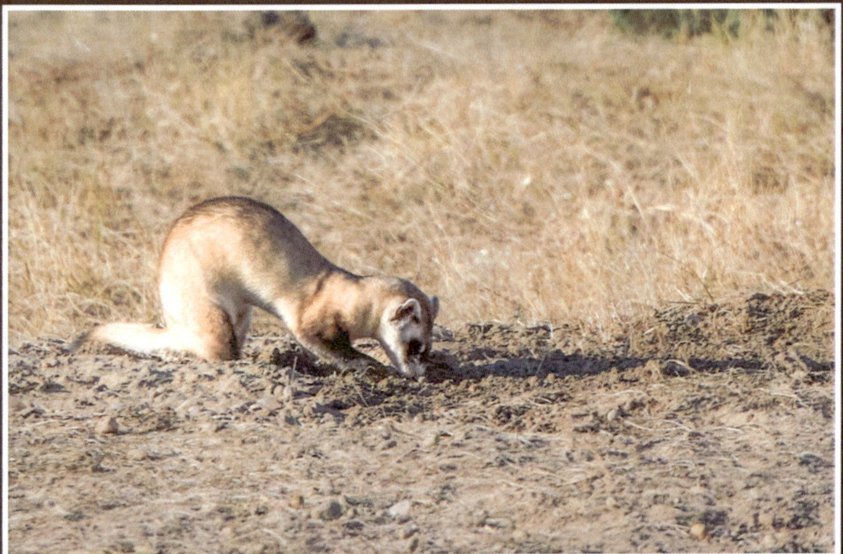

Strong paws help BFFs grab prairie dogs and dig out blockages in prairie dog holes.

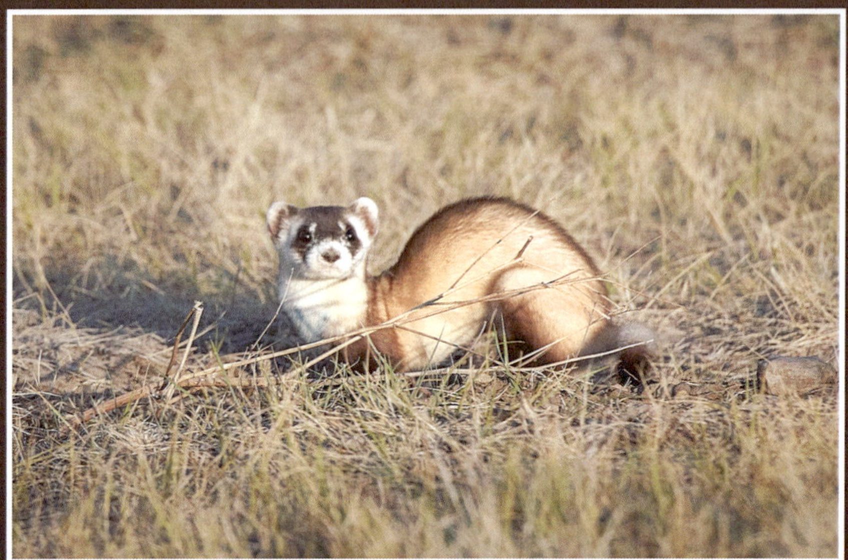

A flexible spine, like a spring, helps with speed and agility.

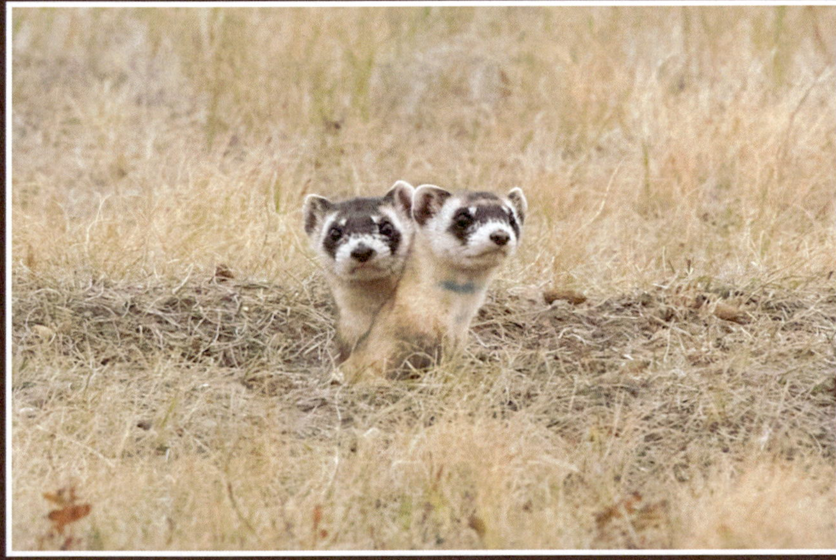

A bandit mask sets them apart. Every BFF's mask has a unique, one-of-a-kind color pattern, like a fingerprint.

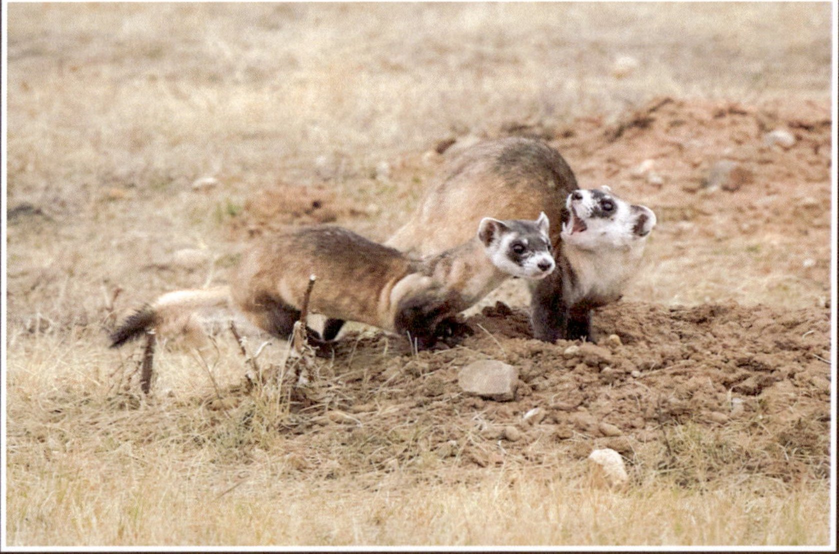

BFFs have the longest canine teeth (fangs) relative to skull size of any carnivorous mammal!

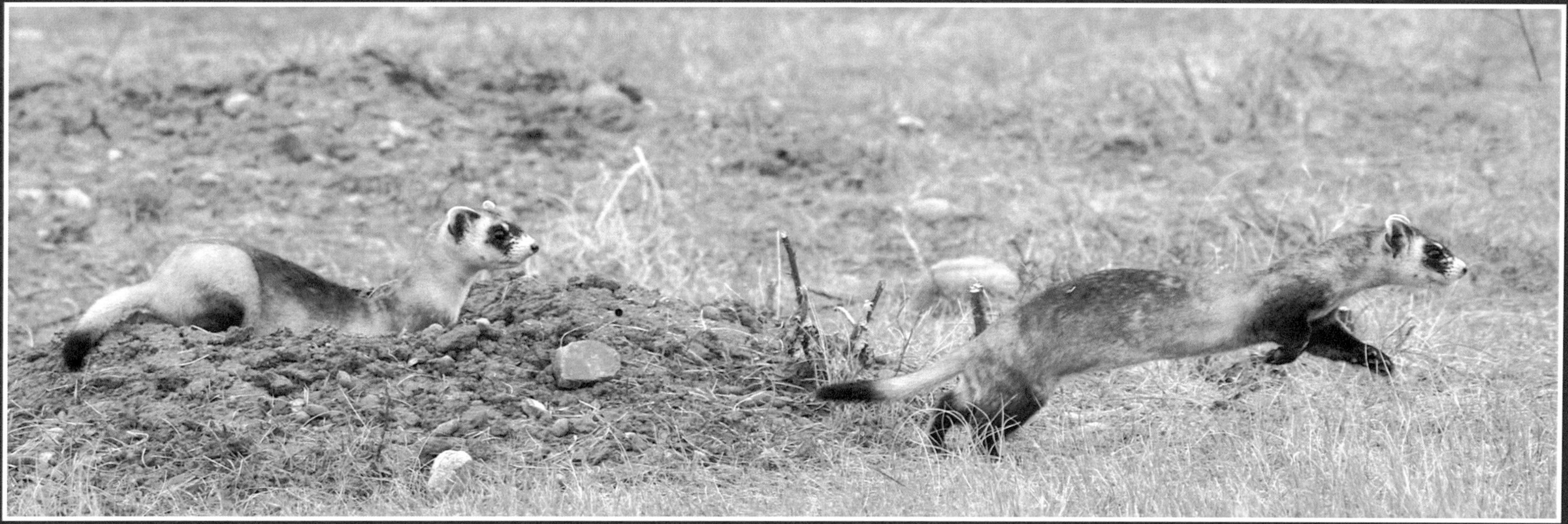

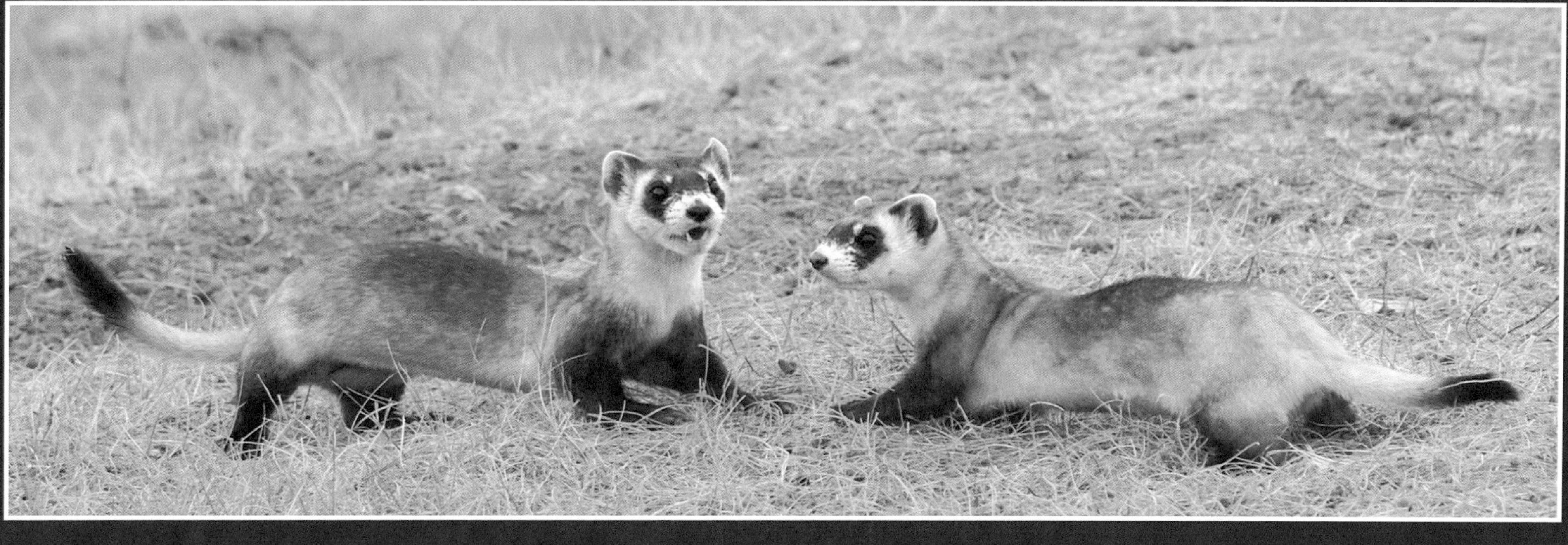

BFFs ARE

born tiny and adorable.

Black-footed ferret kits are born as tiny as a human's pinky finger, with their eyes and ears closed. Coiled together in a warm, snuggly ball, they chitter and cheep for their mother's milk and attention. They are helpless without her.

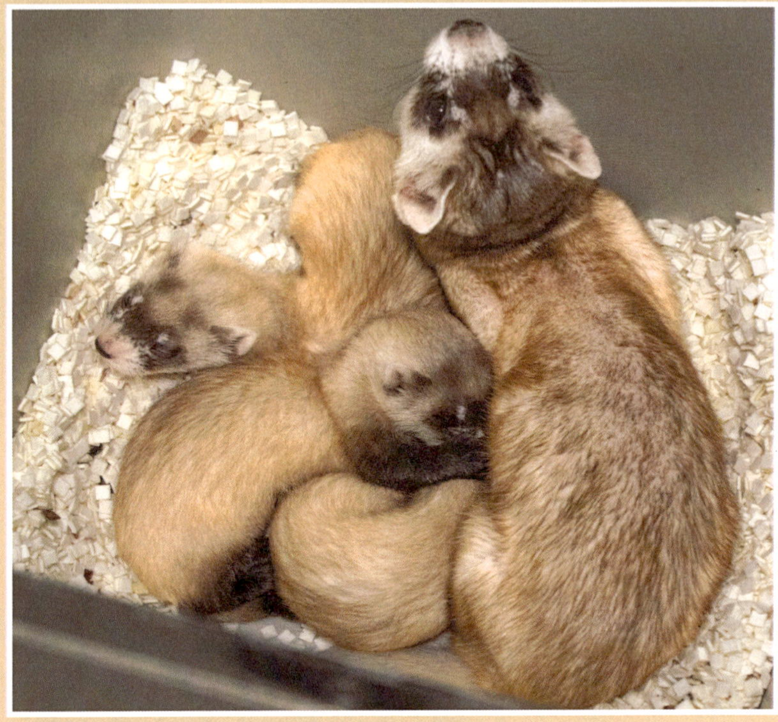

Mother BFF and her forty-day-old kits.

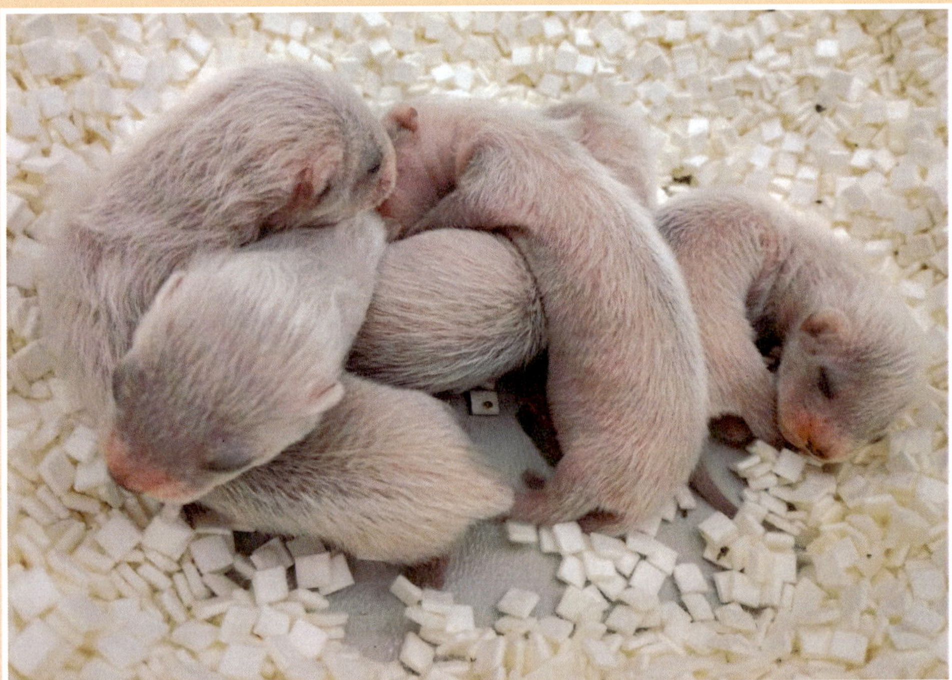

These cuties are newborns. *(Photo by Kimberly Fraser)*

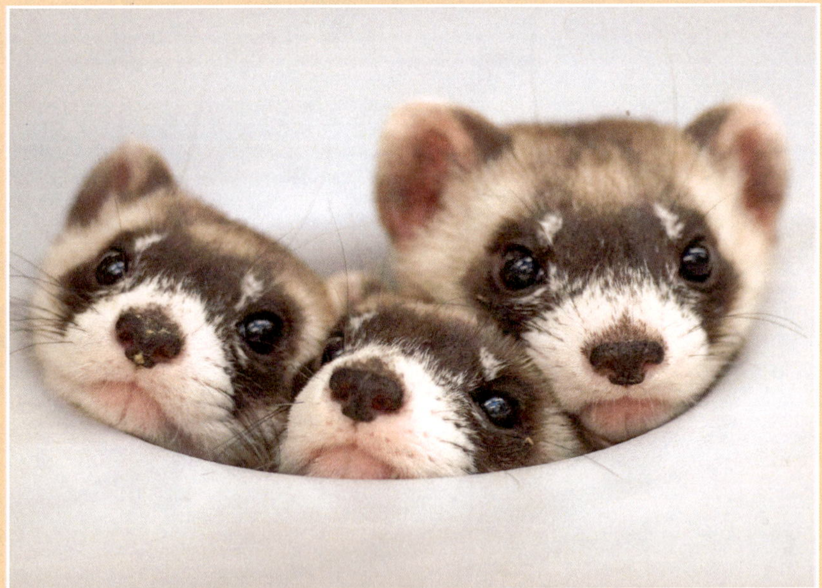

Sixty days old and very curious! *(Photo by Kimberly Fraser)*

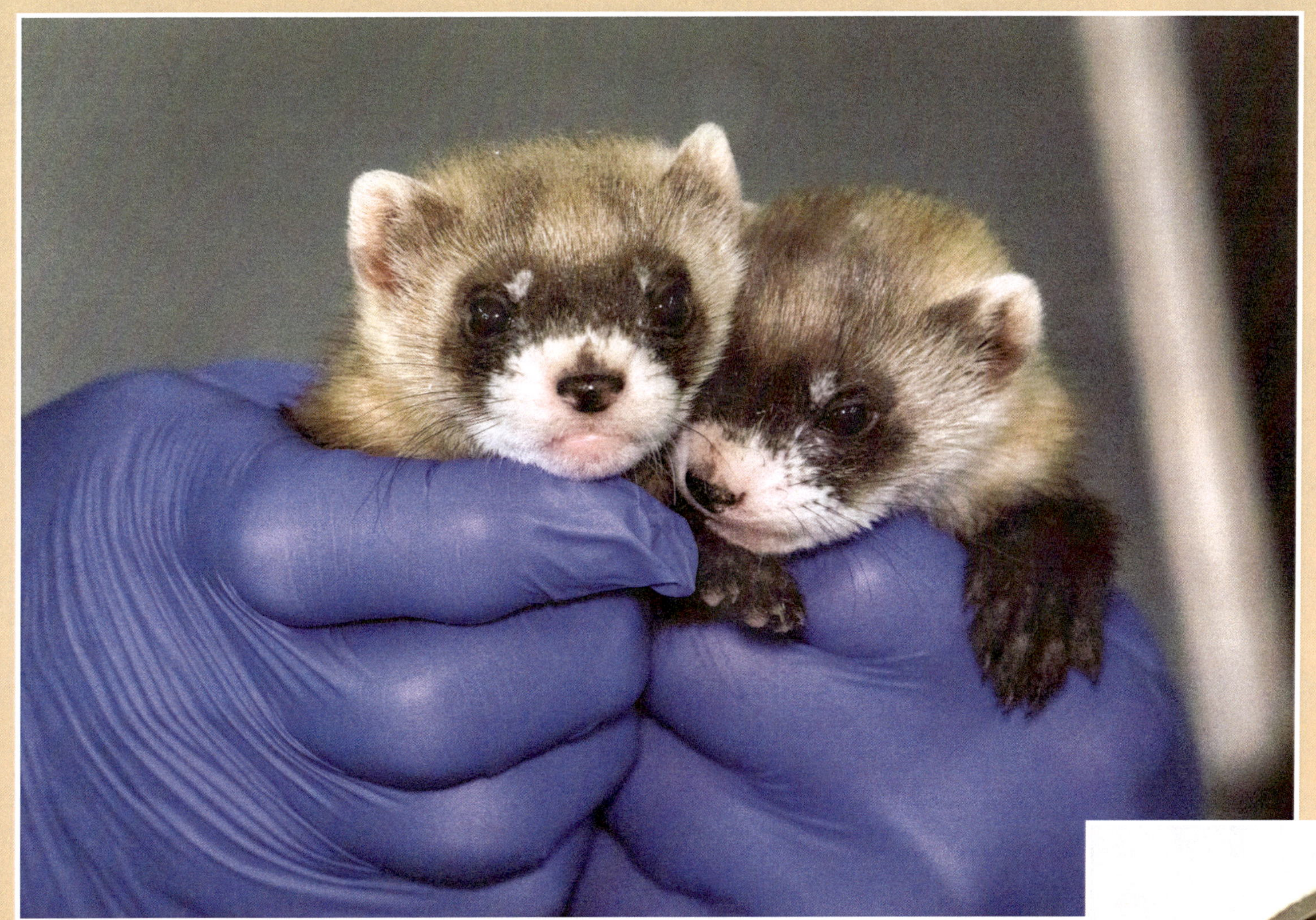

Less than thirty days old with eyes open.

Kits on these pages were born at the US Fish and Wildlife Service (USFWS) National Black-Footed Ferret Conservation Center. (See pages 46–47 for more.)

BFFs ARE

cunning and cautious from a young age.

In nature, black-footed ferret moms raise their kits in a safe, comfy den at the bottom of prairie dog holes, eight to twelve feet belowground. By the time their kits are sixty days old, moms have brought them their first taste of prairie dog, which imprints on them that prairie dogs are the food they need to hunt. Soon kits begin exploring the aboveground world, never far from their den.

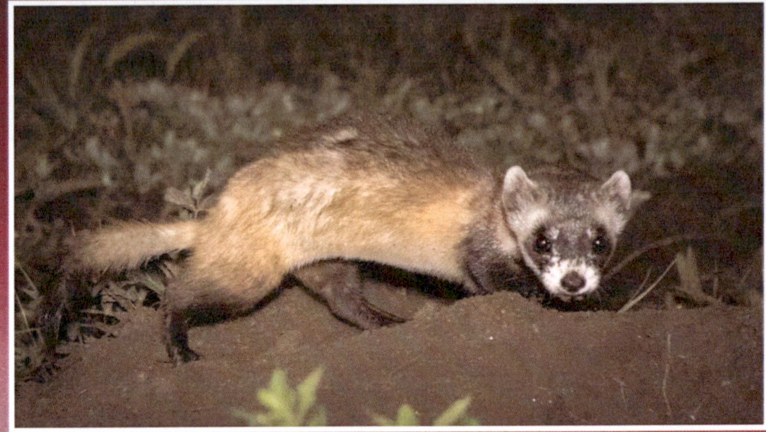

Wild-born black-footed ferret kit, three and a half months old.

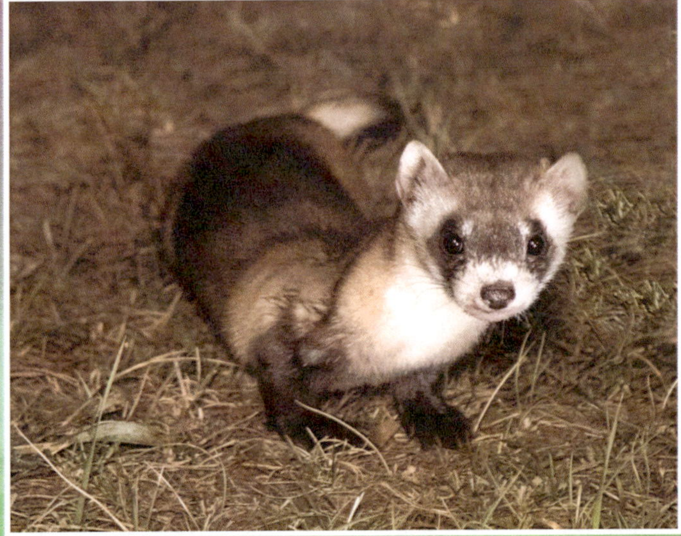

Wild-born black-footed ferret kit, four and a half months old.

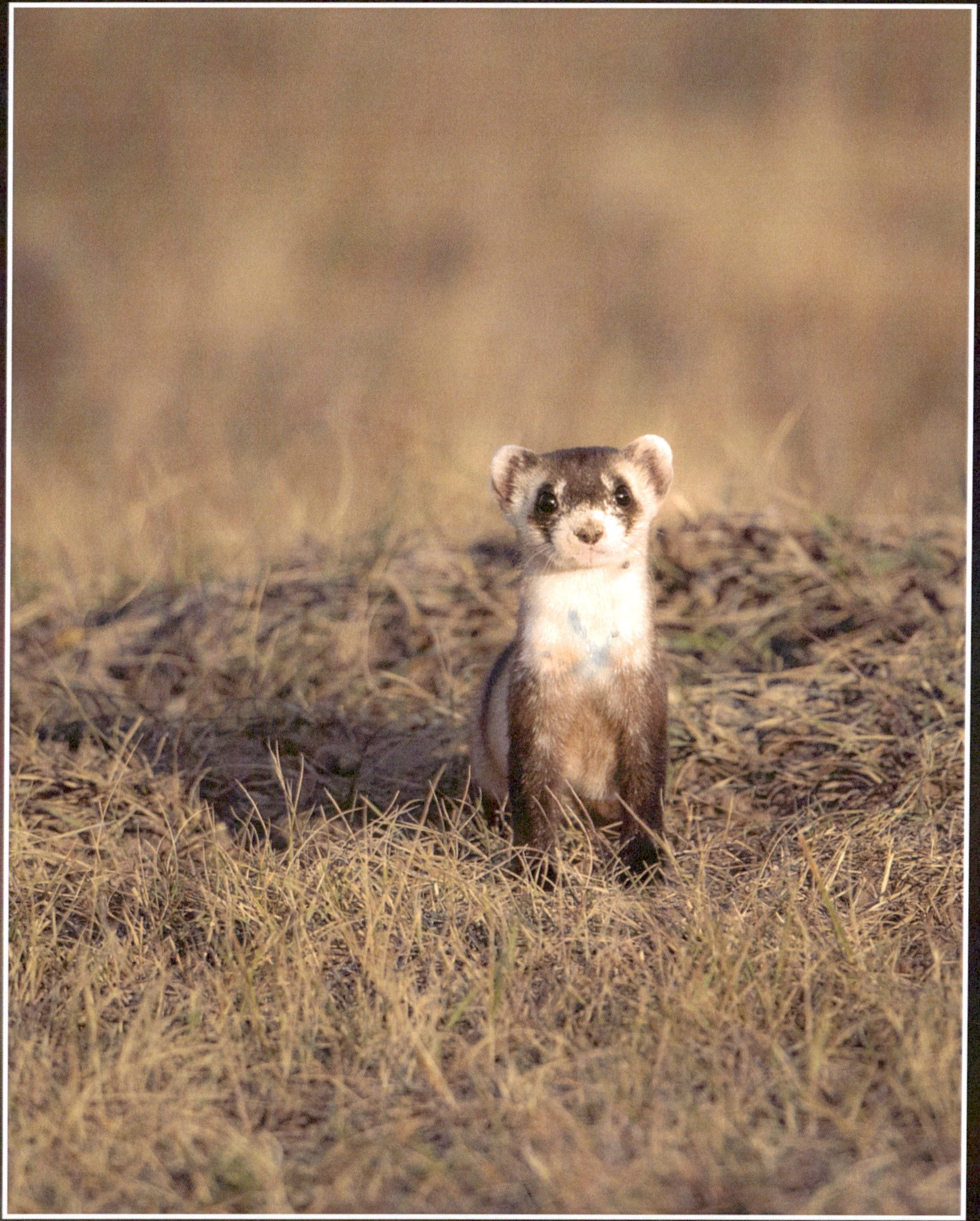

This wild-born kit is five months old. The temporary blue mark on her fur shows she was just vaccinated, which is important for saving black-footed ferrets. (See pages 44–45.)

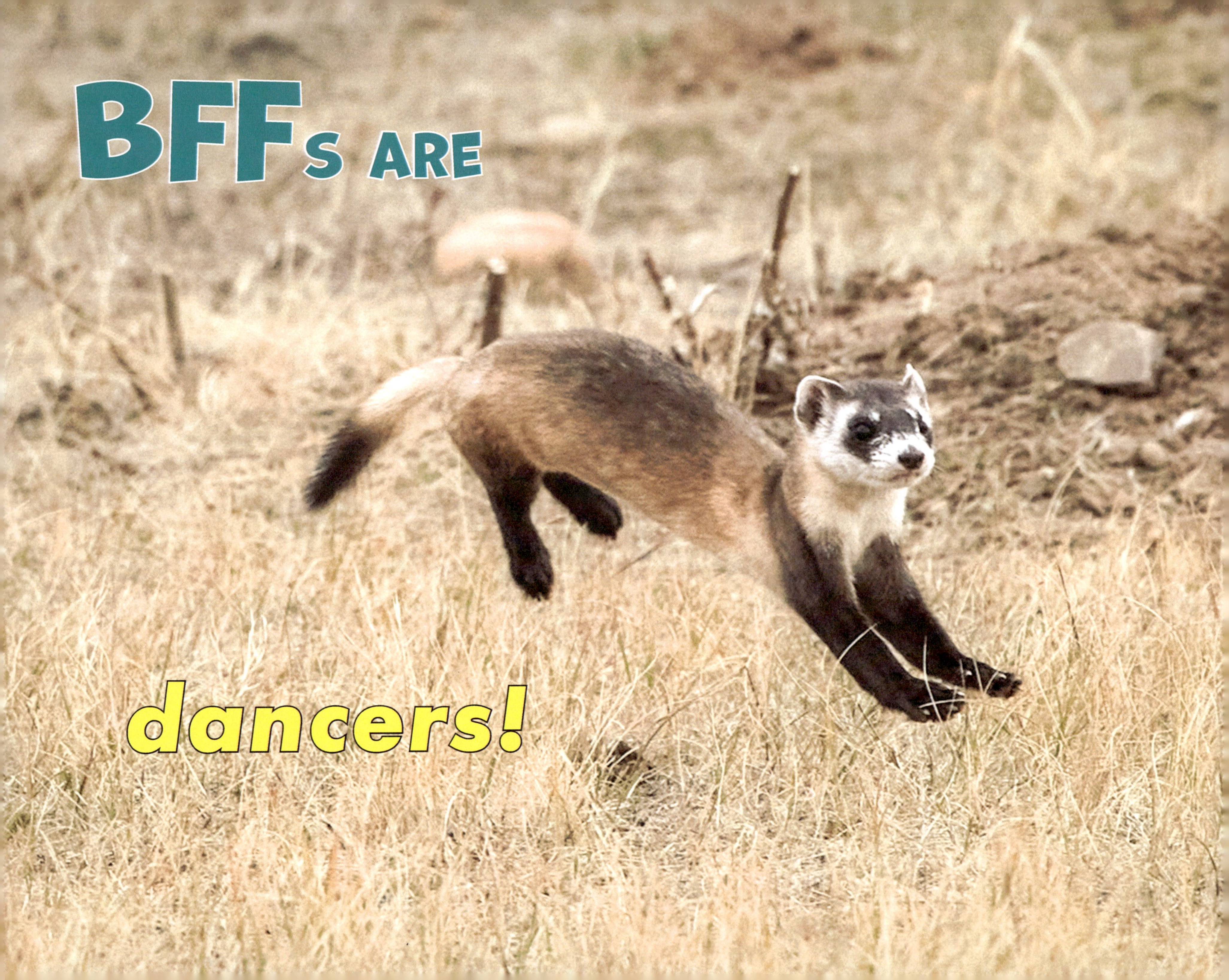

BFFs ARE
dancers!

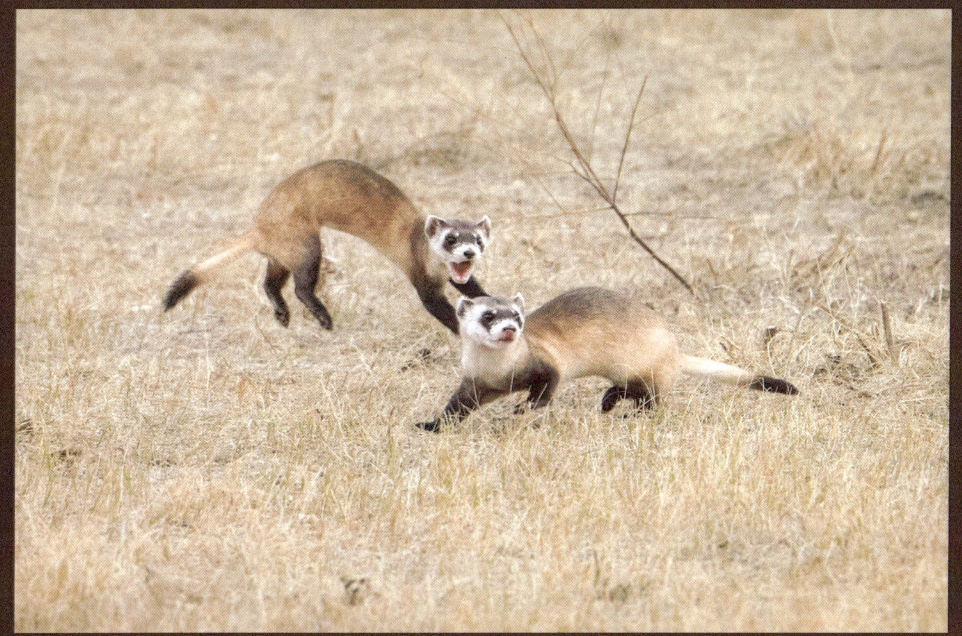

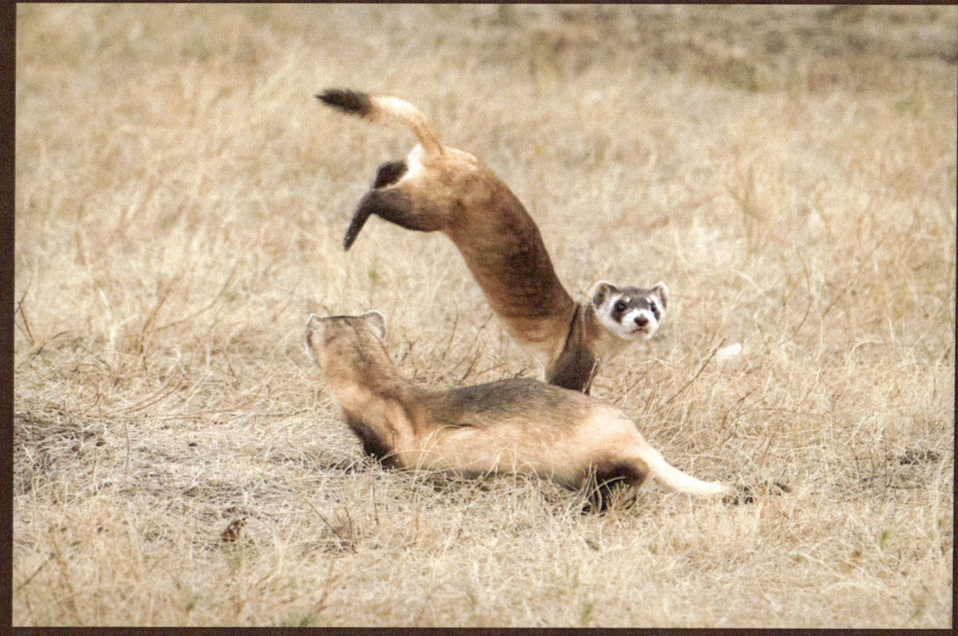

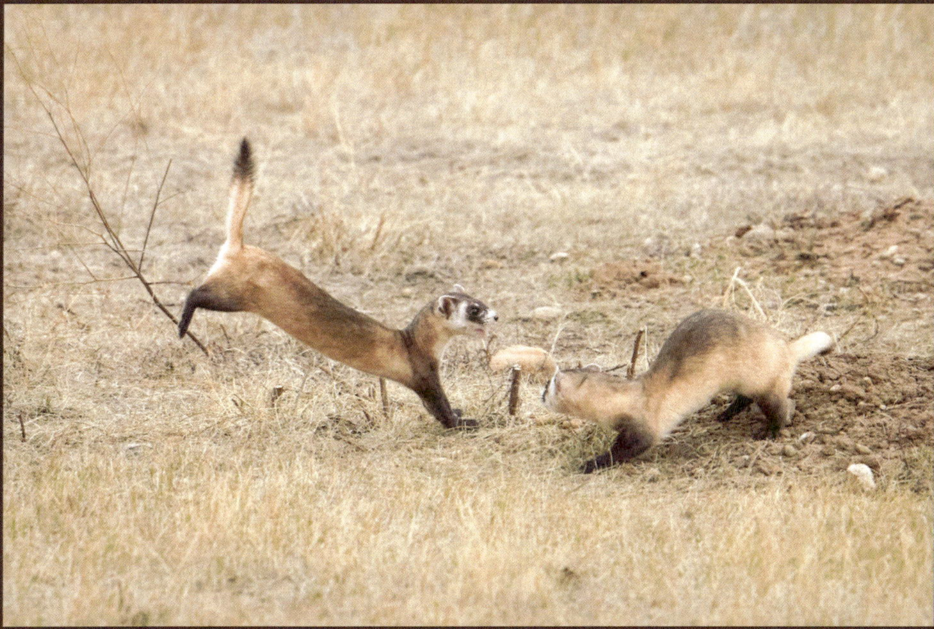

Shortly after black-footed ferret kits learn to walk, they begin to dance! Dancing is both a fun and safe way to learn agility, hunting skills, and self-defense.

During the play-dance, BFFs take turns charging toward one another in a pretend attack. They might bark, hiss, or make chit-chit-chittering sounds, then dive down a prairie dog hole. They usually dance at night but have also been seen dancing after rainstorms. Might the pitter patter of raindrops start the pitter patter of tiny black feet?

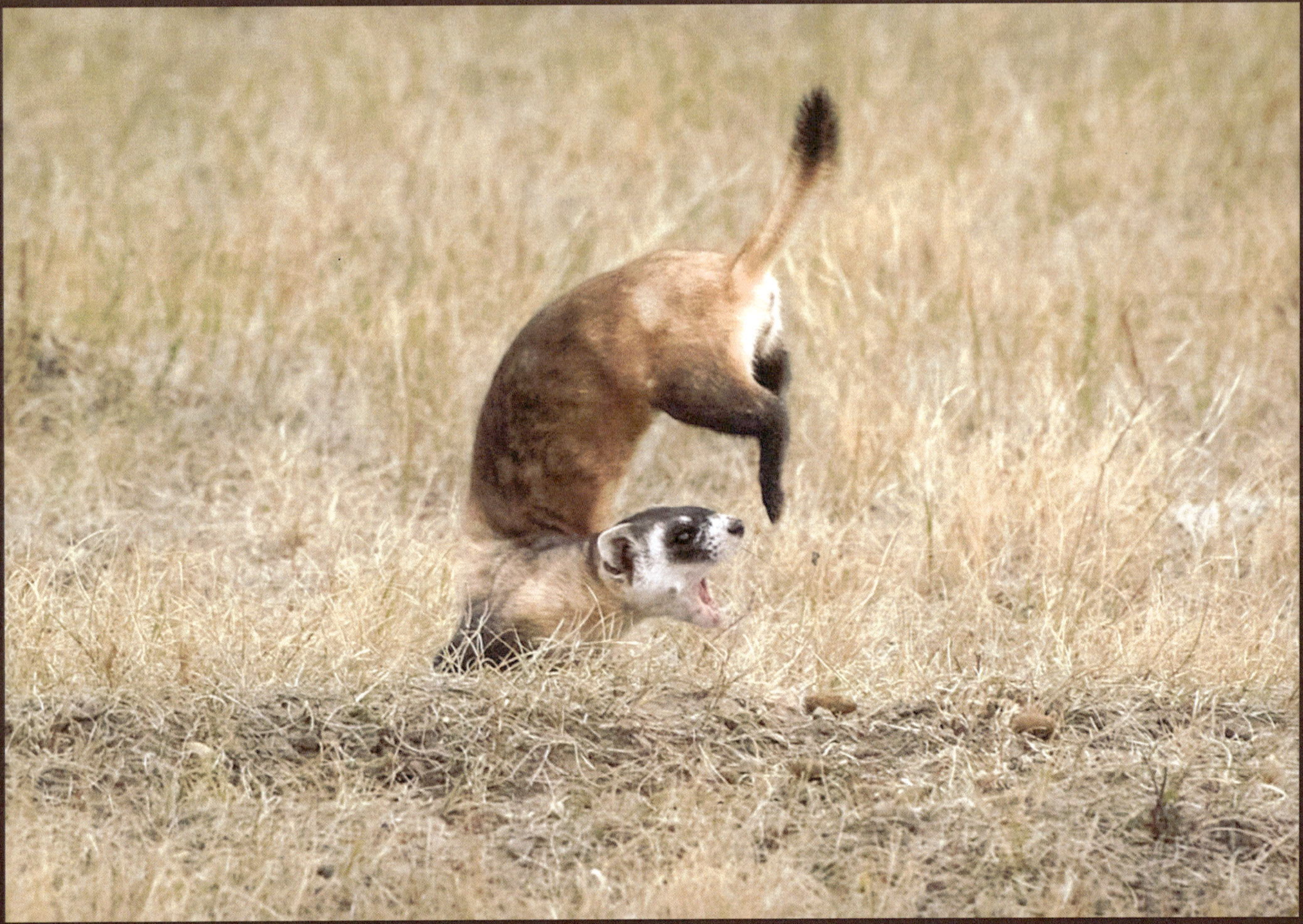

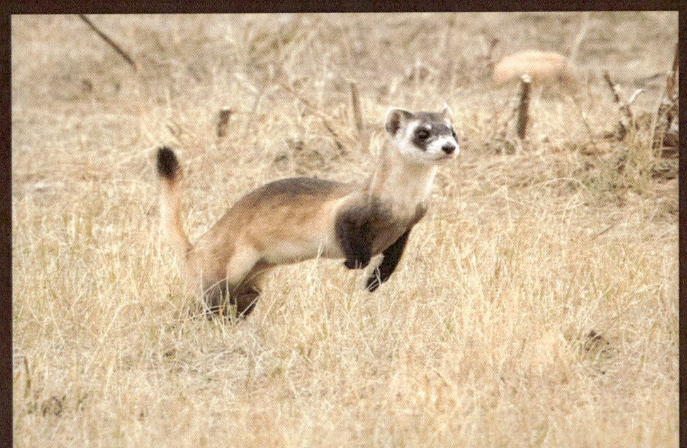
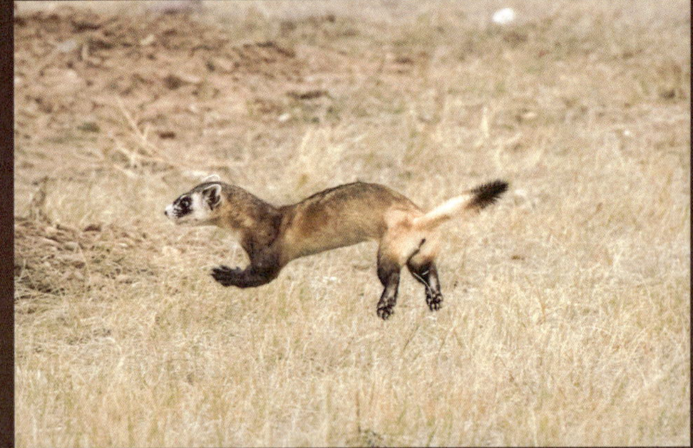
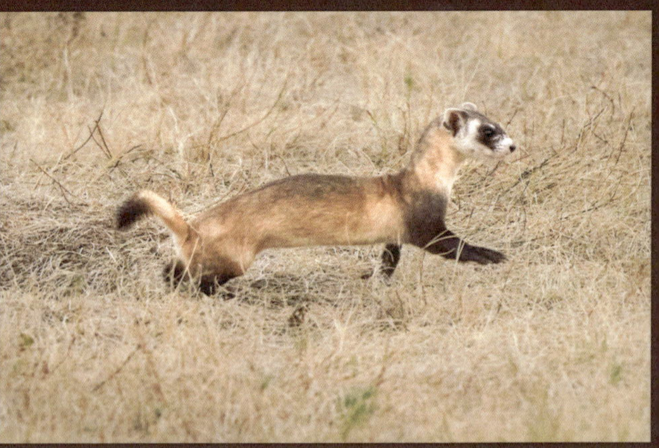

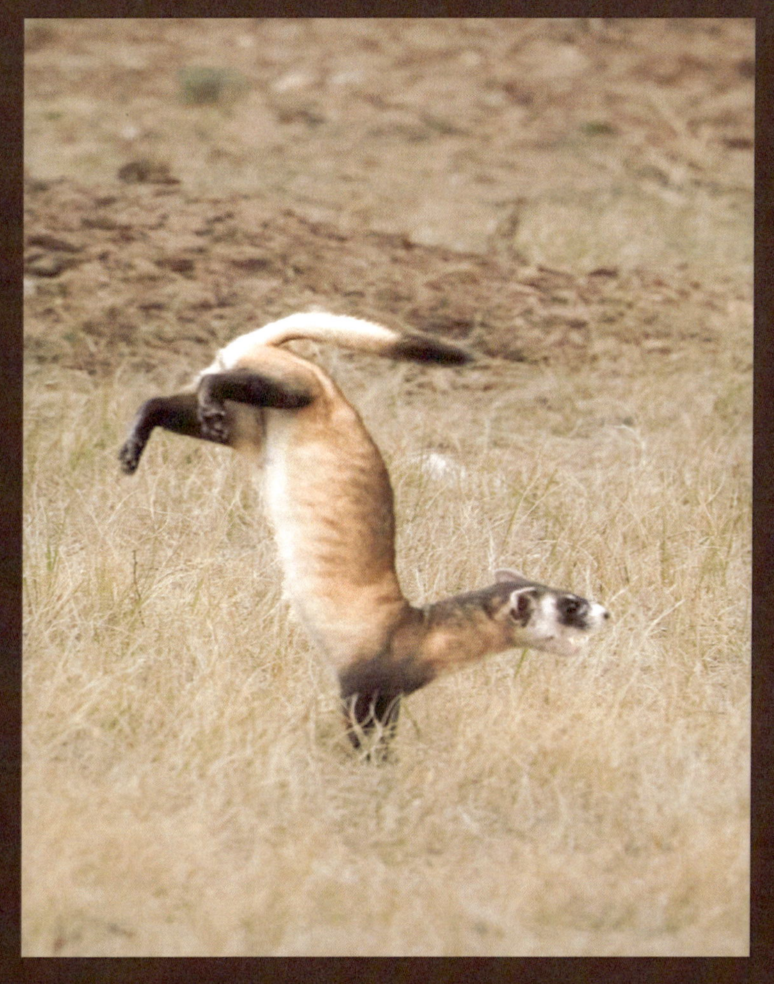
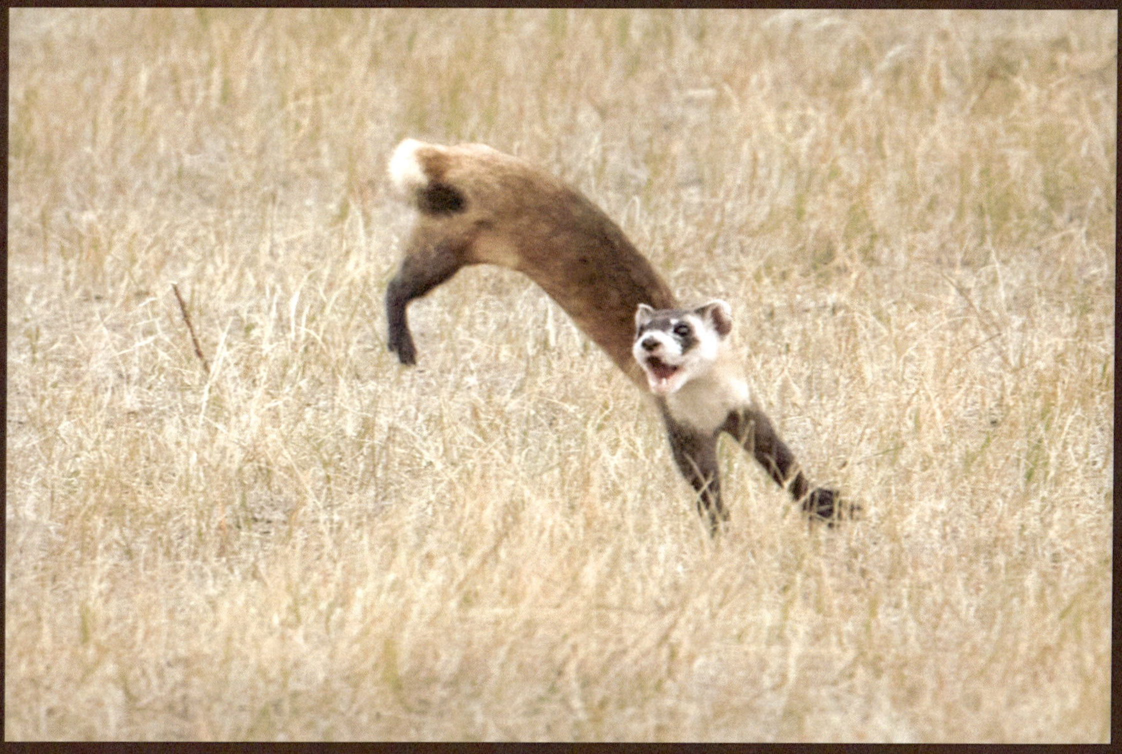
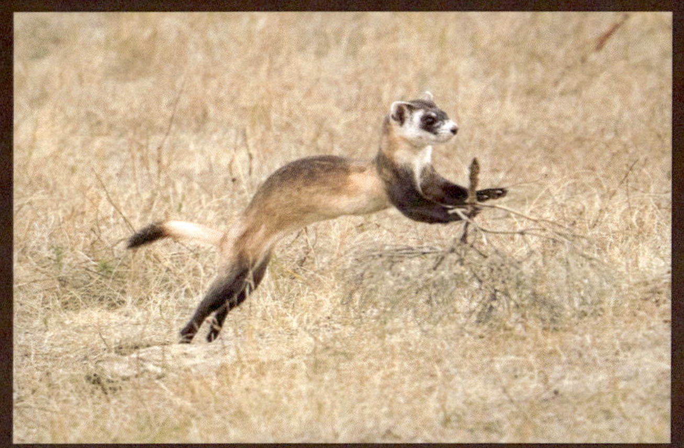
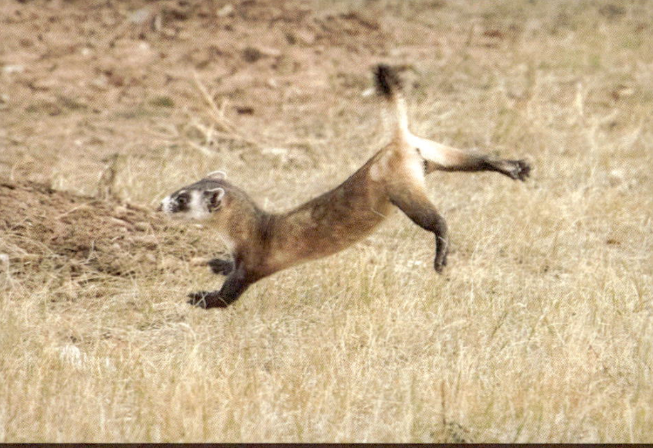
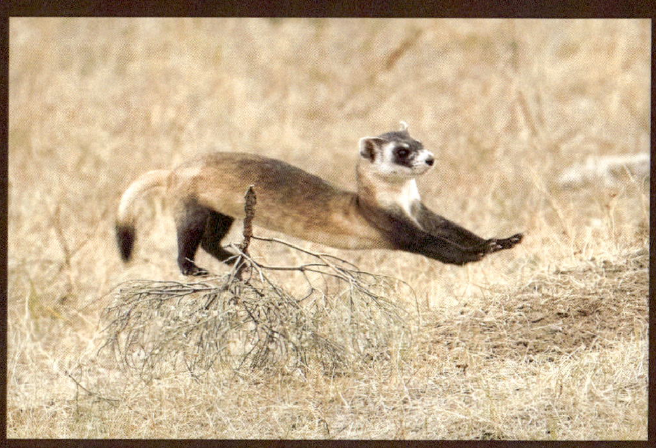

BFFs ARE

oh, so curious.

Black-footed ferrets often stretch up tall and watch their surroundings. We call this periscoping. They keep a close eye on other BFFs in their territories. Most importantly, they periscope to look out for danger.

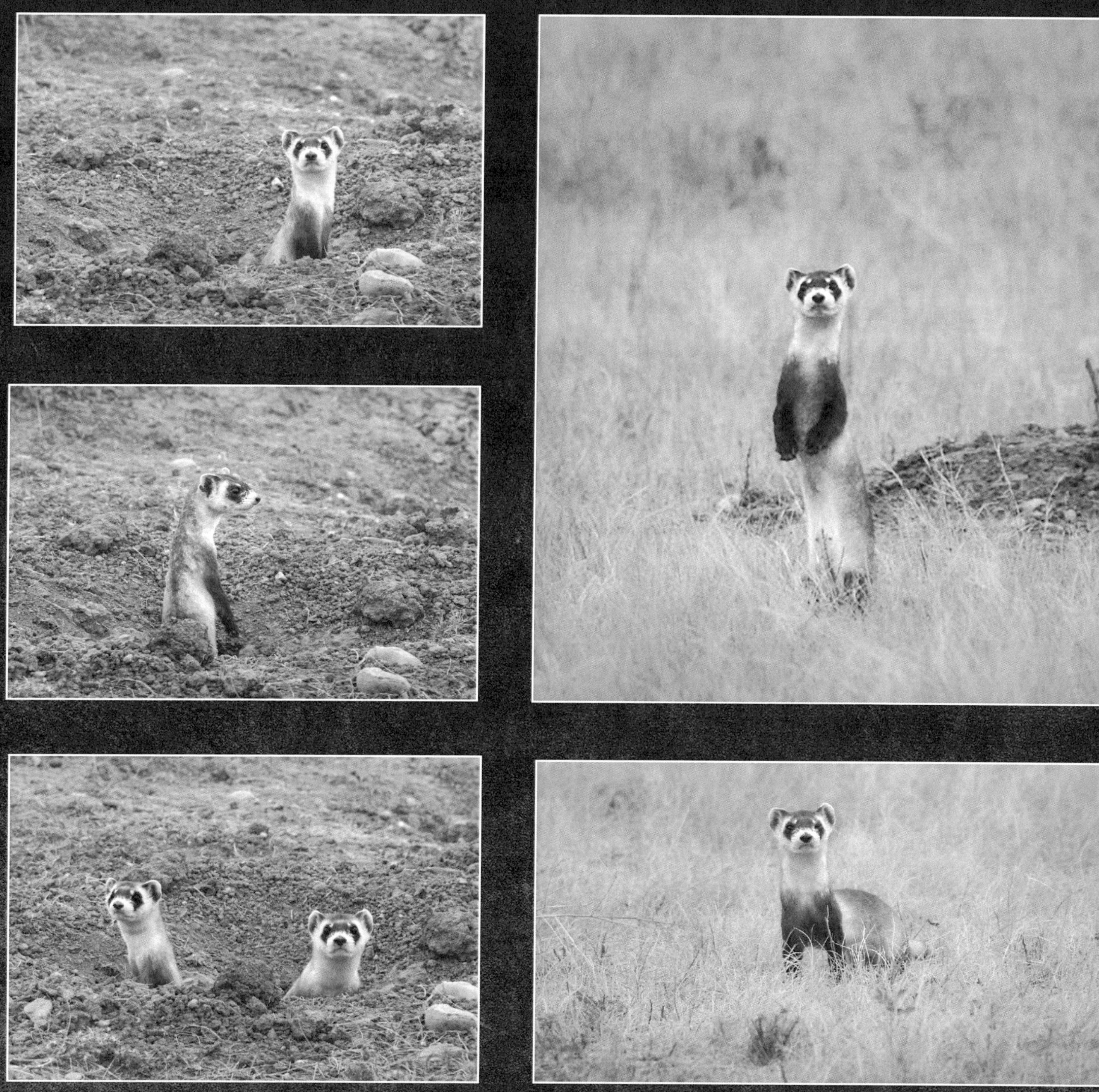

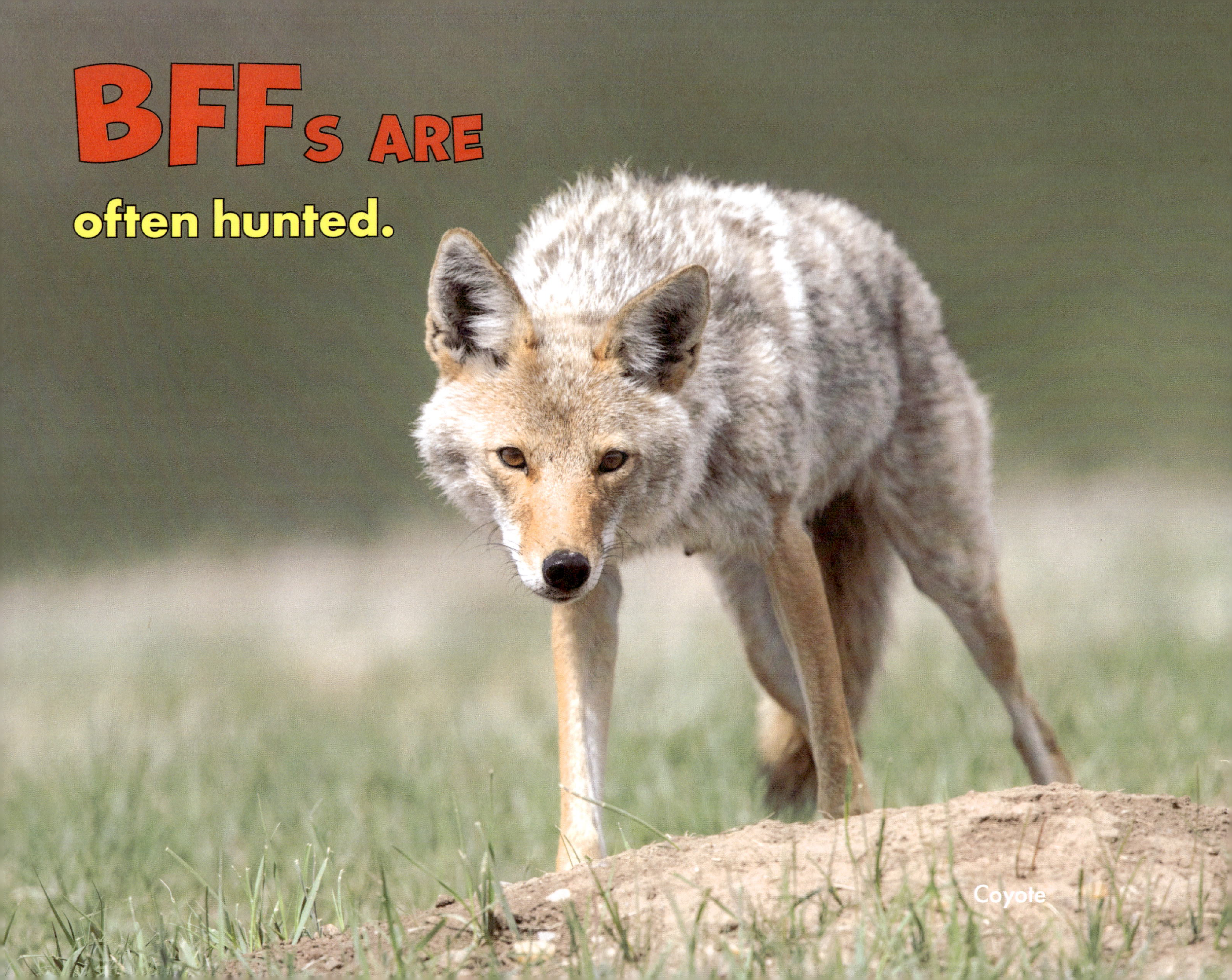

BFFs ARE
often hunted.
Coyote

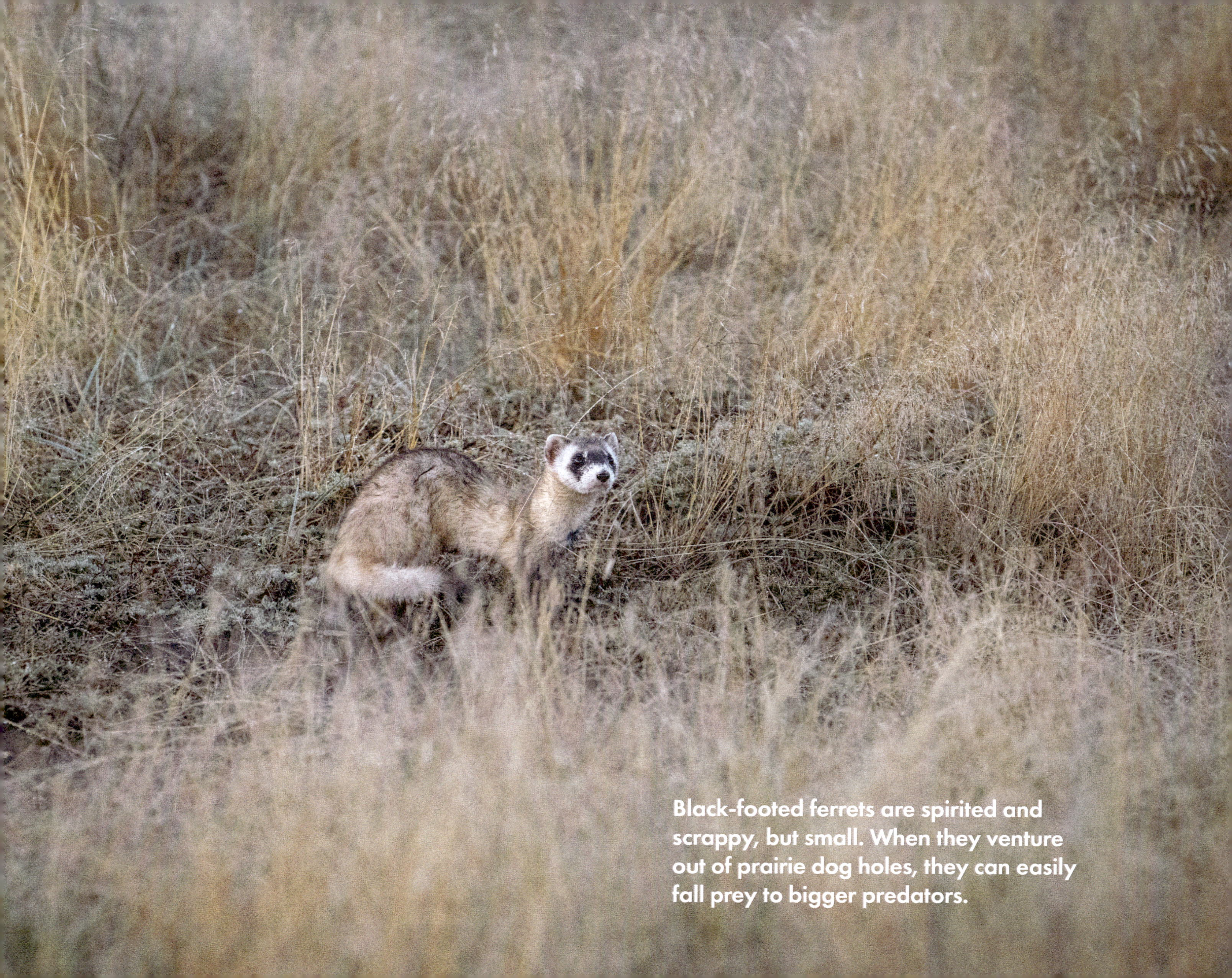
Black-footed ferrets are spirited and scrappy, but small. When they venture out of prairie dog holes, they can easily fall prey to bigger predators.

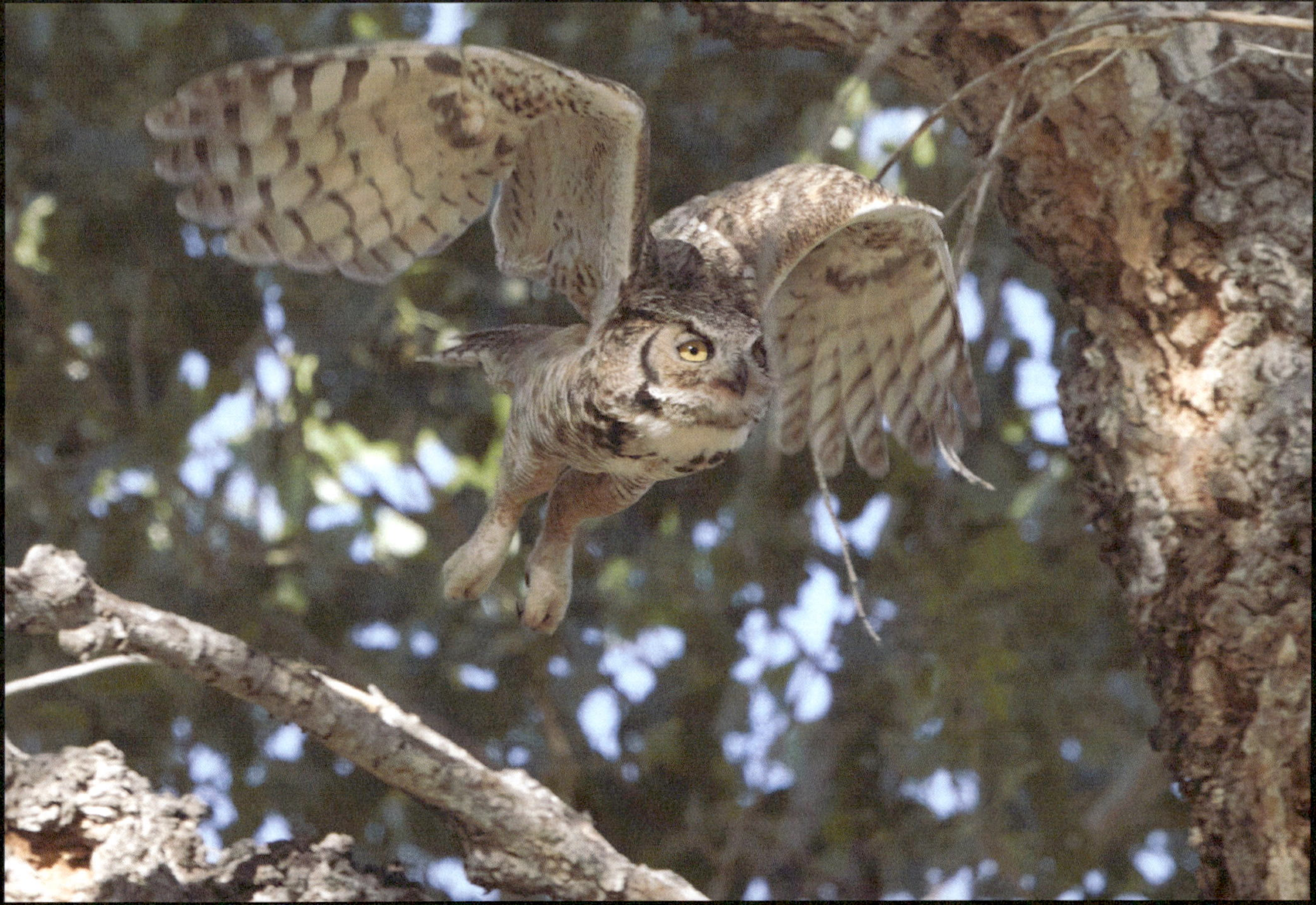

Great-horned owl

PREDATORS
Coyote (page 34)
American badger
Great-horned owl
Gray fox
Bobcat

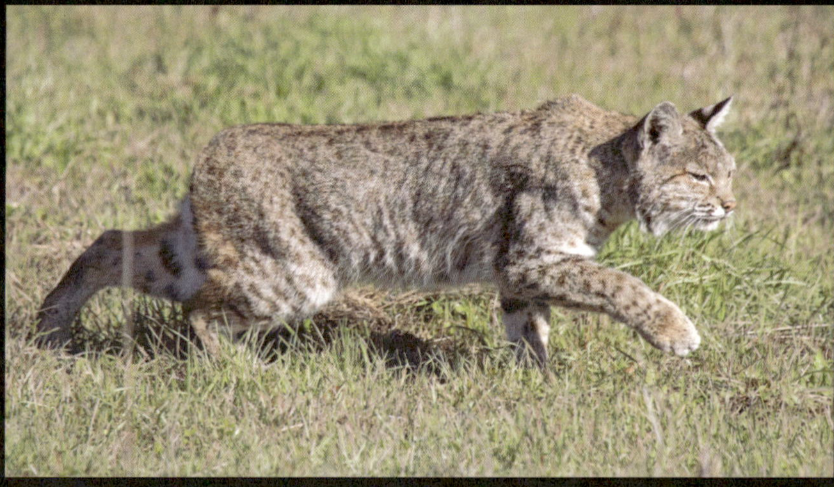

Bobcat

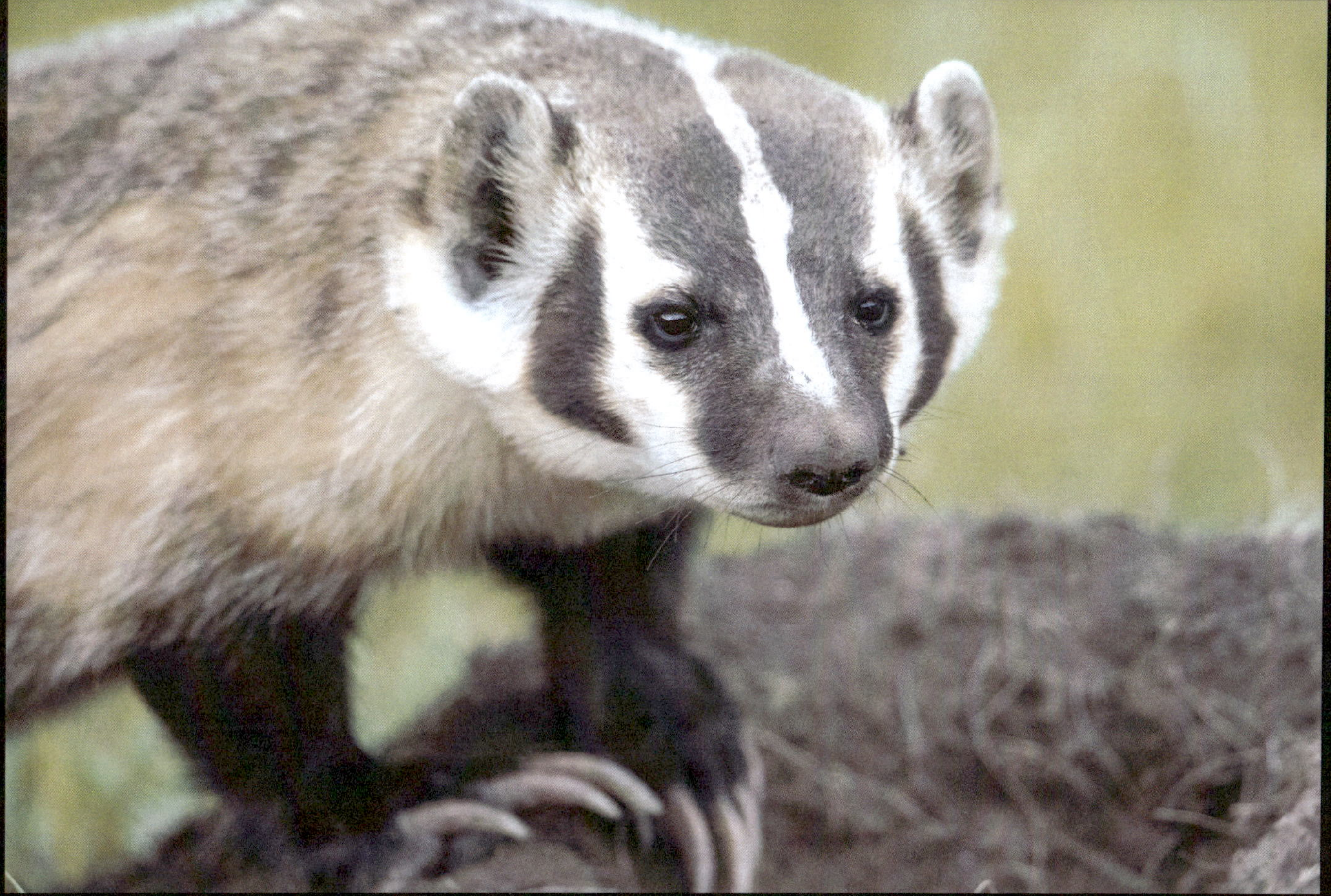

American badger

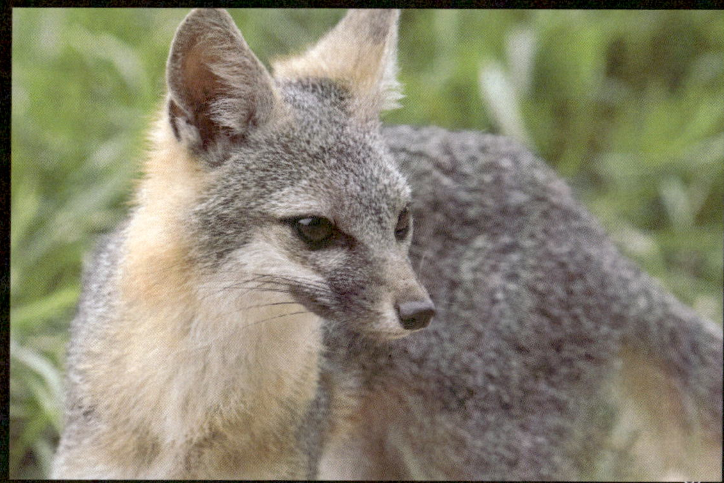

Gray fox

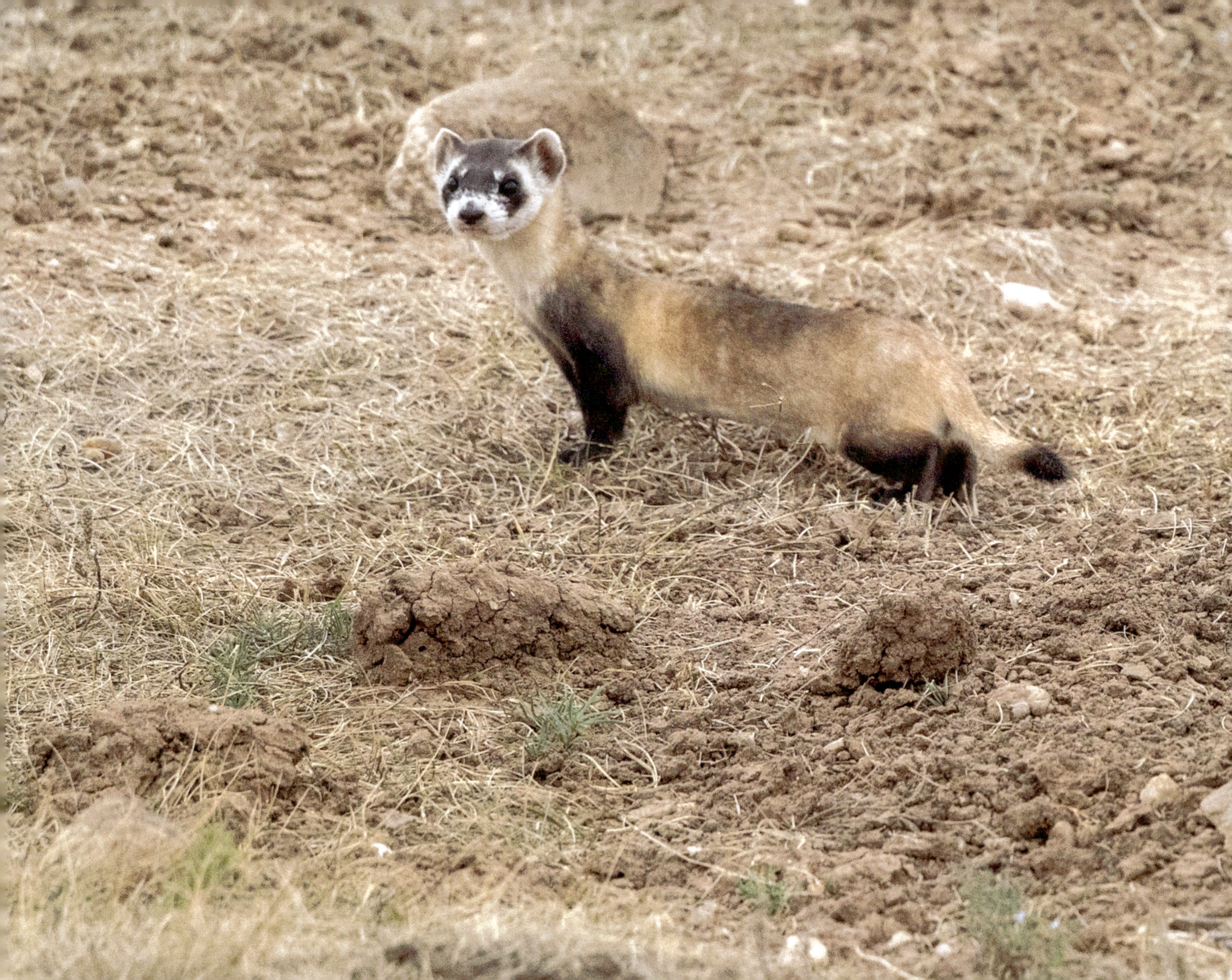

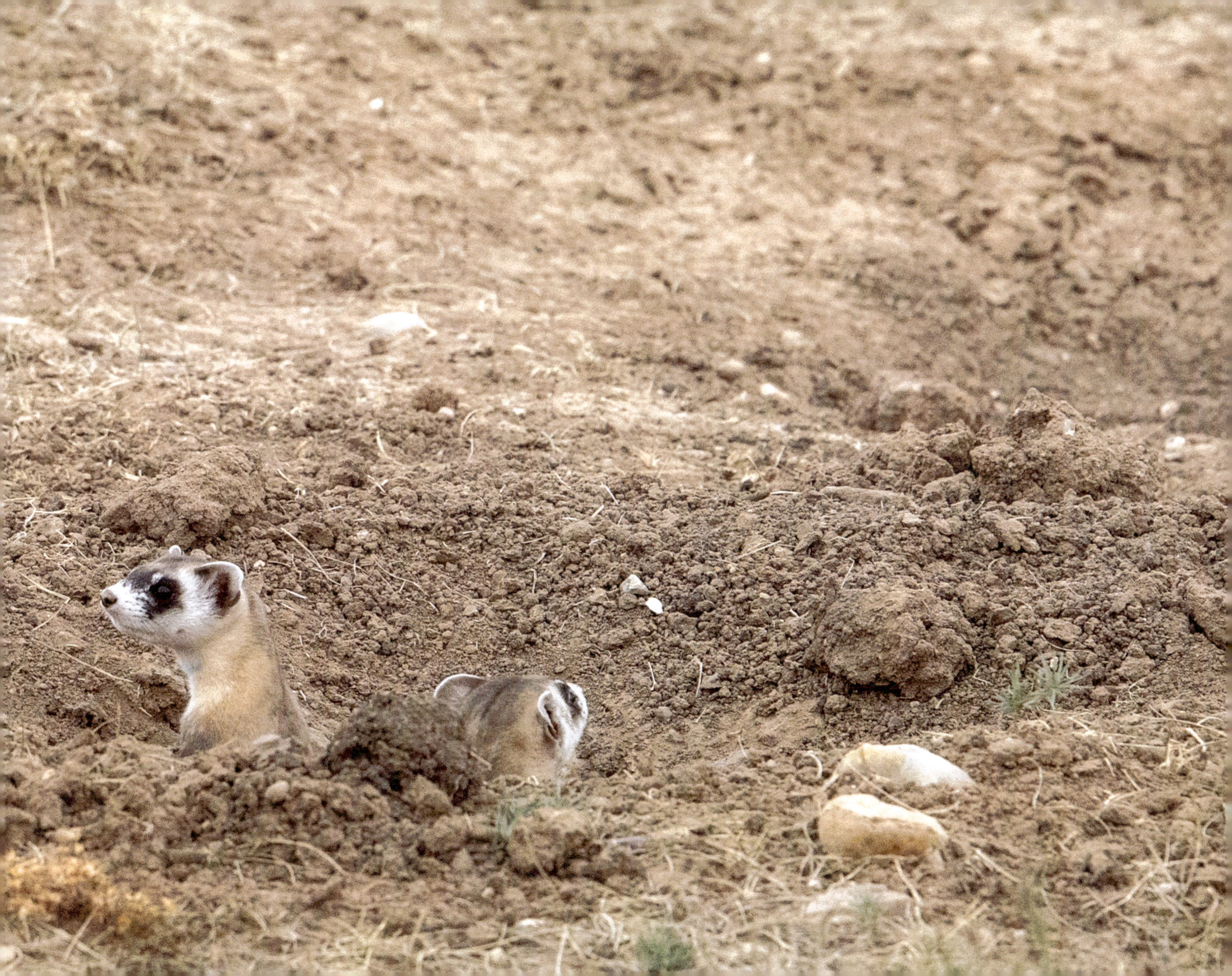

BFFs ARE fiercely independent.

Around five months old, black-footed ferret kits have learned to be ferocious hunters and to perform other important ferret life skills. Now they disperse, moving away from home.

Young male BFFs may disperse up to four miles away, if they can find safe habitat.

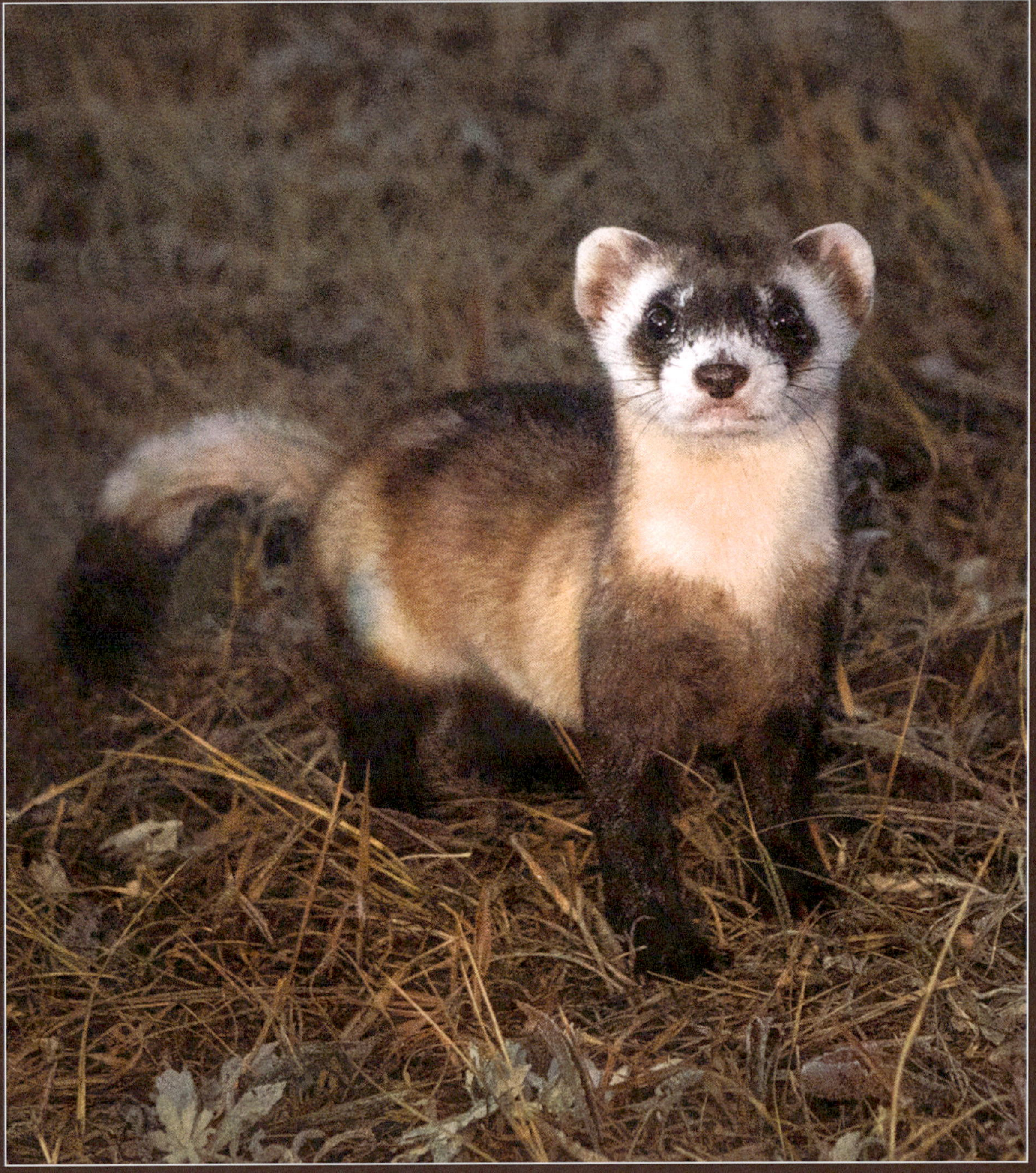

Young female BFFs disperse, too. But they tend to stay closer to Mom and may even share her territory. Here, a mother tenderly nibbles the back of her daughter's neck for the last time.

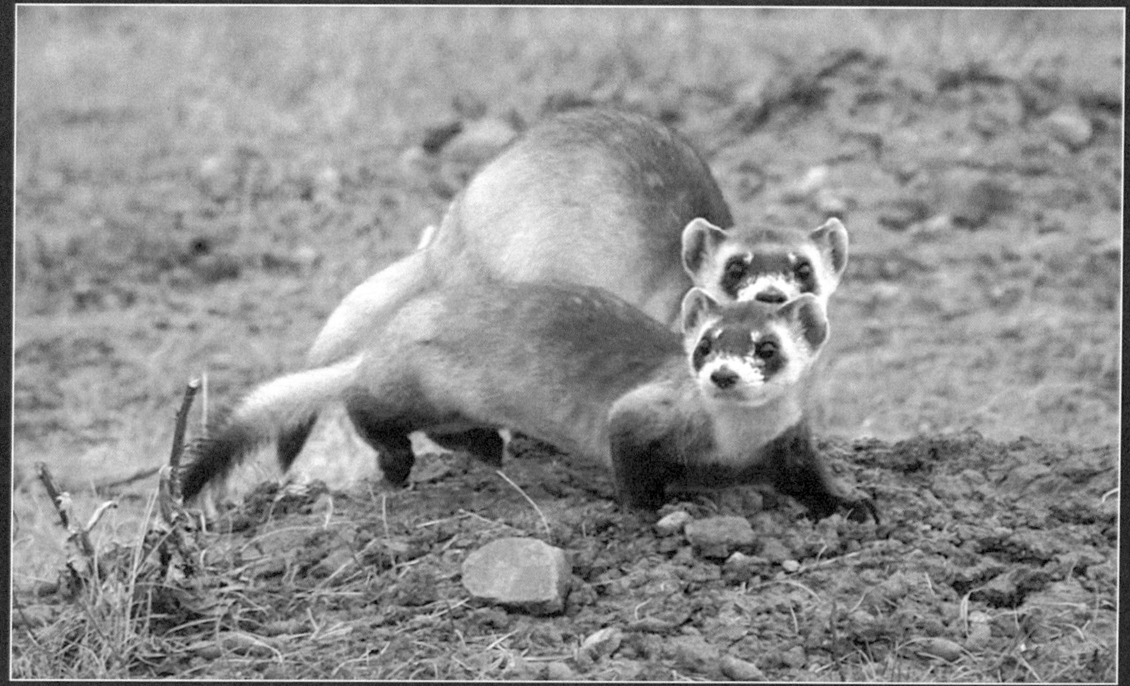

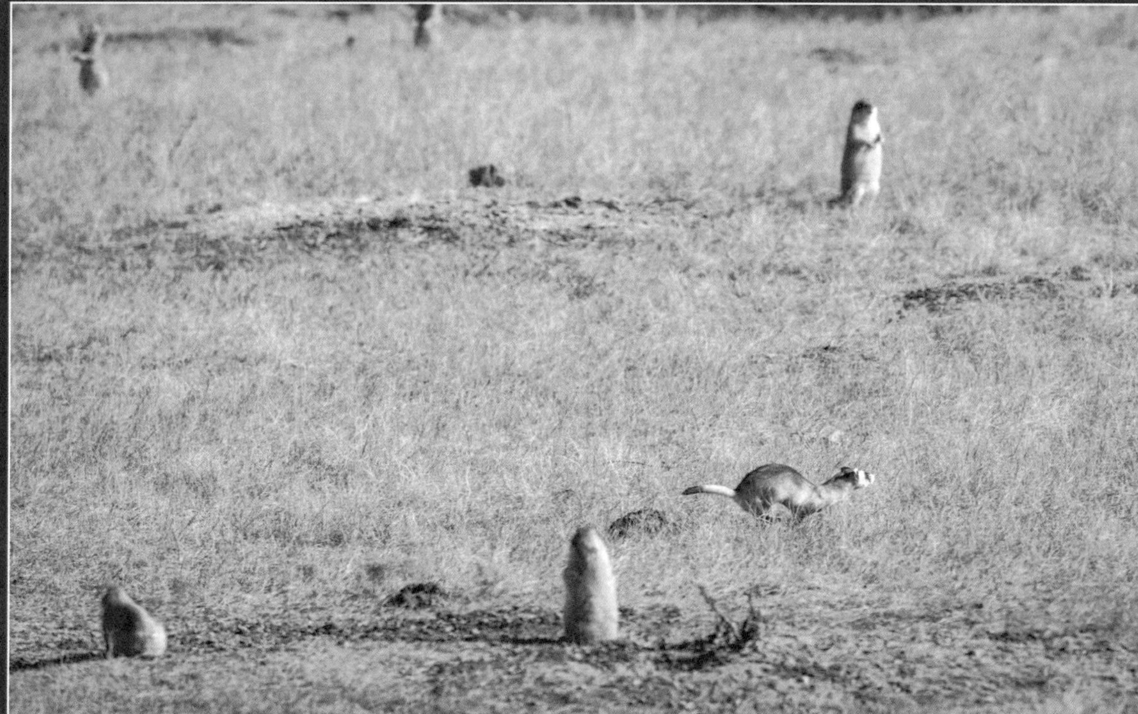

Then, her little girl makes a sudden dash across the prairie dog colony.

Will she scamper back home to Mom or keep running into the distance?

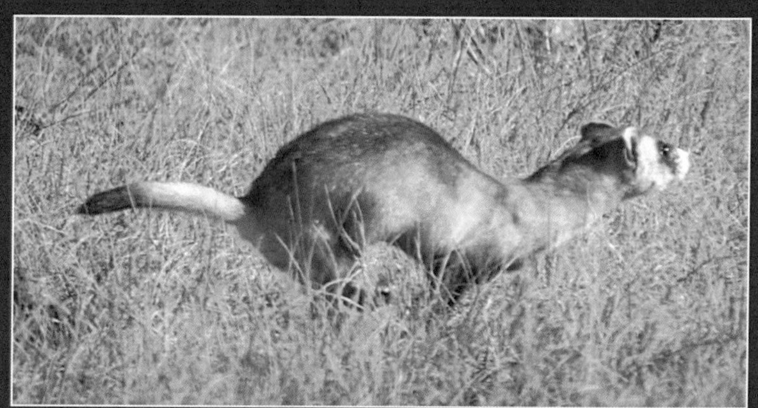

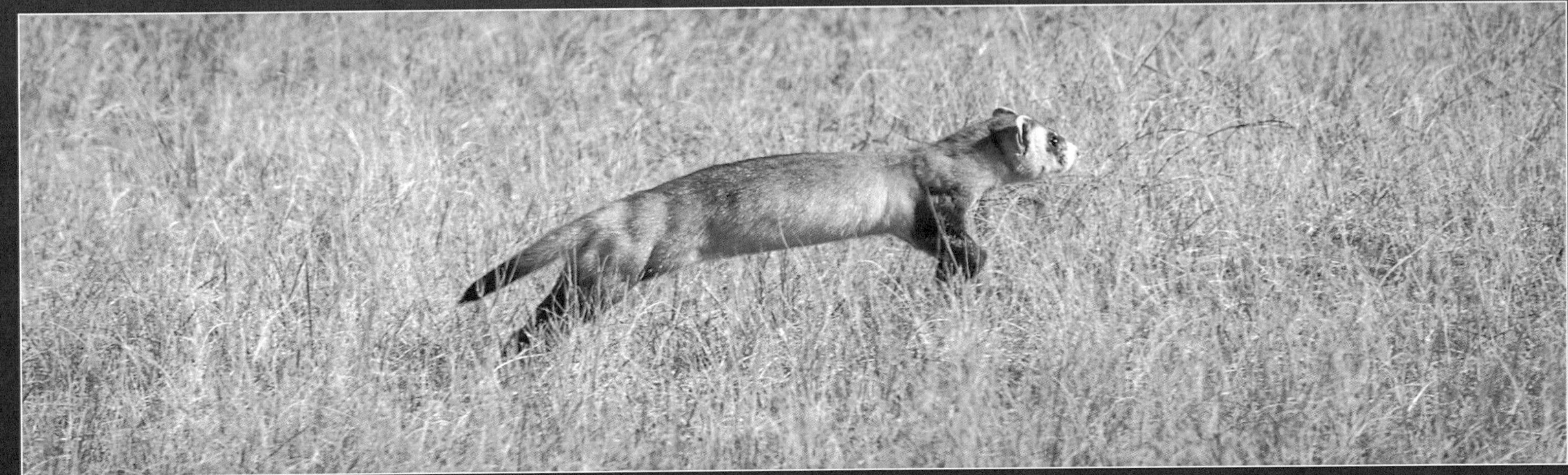

The kit boldly leaps away—off to new adventures.

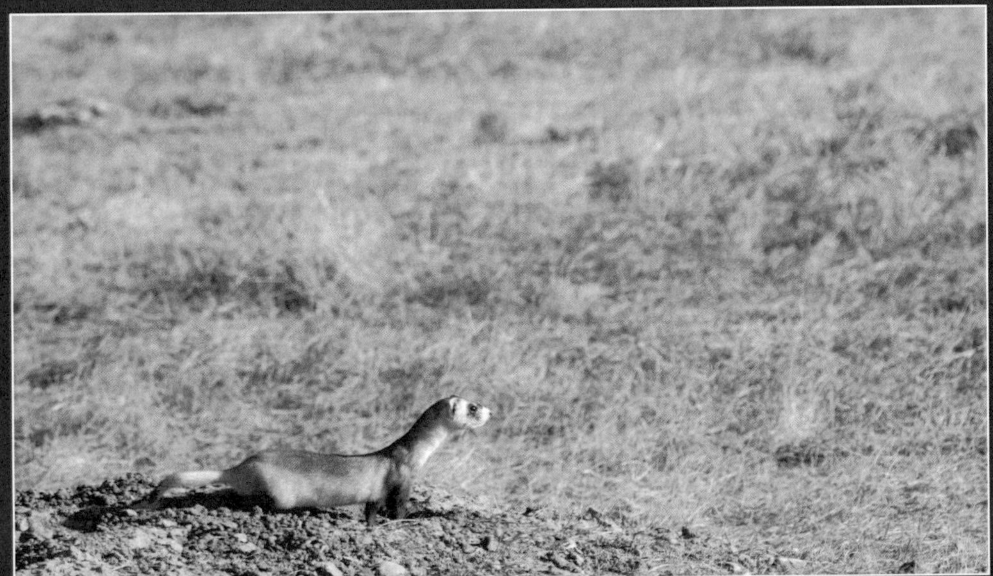

Mom gazes at her nearly grown-up daughter, now far away across the colony.

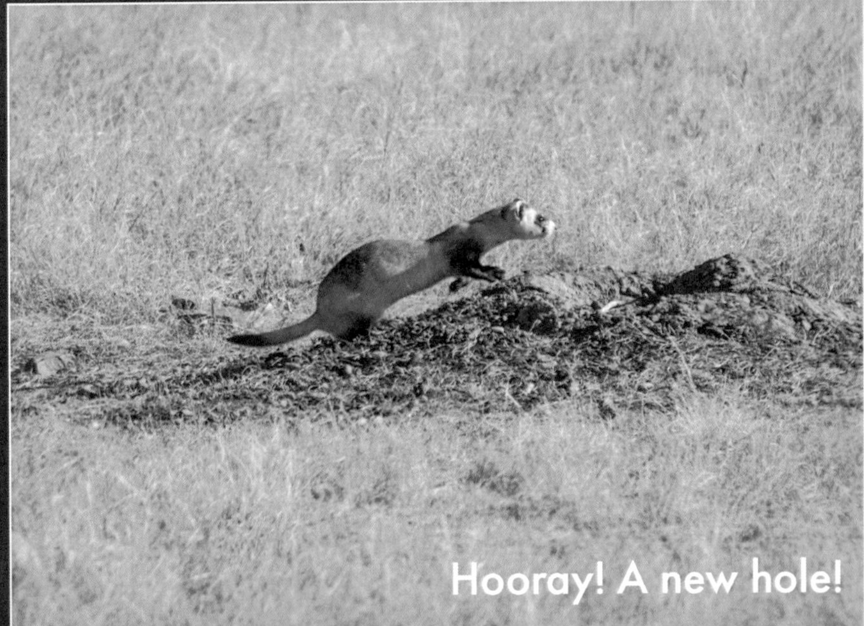

Hooray! A new hole!

The young BFF settles into her new home.

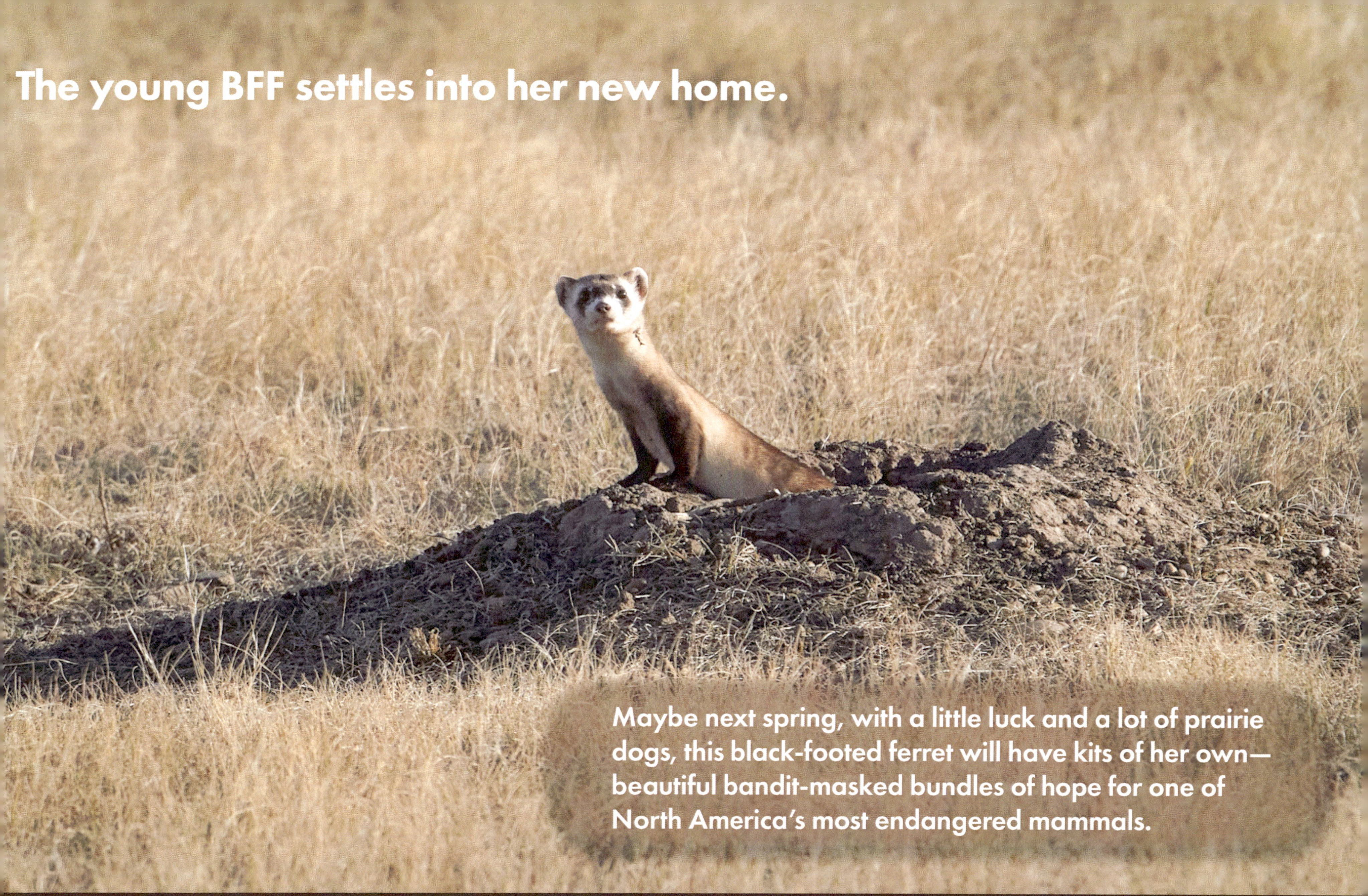

Maybe next spring, with a little luck and a lot of prairie dogs, this black-footed ferret will have kits of her own— beautiful bandit-masked bundles of hope for one of North America's most endangered mammals.

BFFs ARE doing all they can to survive.

BLACK-FOOTED FERRETS NEED OUR HELP

Scientific Name: *Mustela nigripes* — Conservation Status: Endangered

To Save Black-Footed Ferrets, We Must Also Save Prairie Dogs

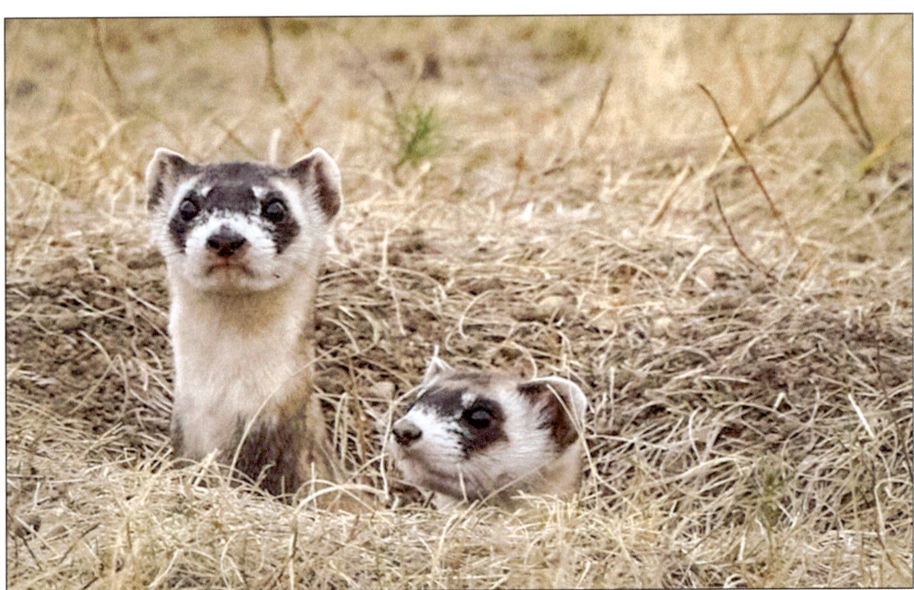

Without prairie dogs, black-footed ferrets simply cannot survive. Prairie dogs serve as the ferrets' primary source of food, and their colonies are the ferrets' only habitat.

Before the 1800s, up to five billion prairie dogs—that's 5,000,000,000—lived on the American prairies from Canada to Mexico. But now, **98 percent of prairie dogs are gone,** and their colonies are small and spread apart. Reasons for the loss: conversion of natural grasslands to farmland, the widespread killing of millions of prairie dogs due to misconceptions that they are "pests" (which sadly continues today), and the introduced disease, sylvatic plague.

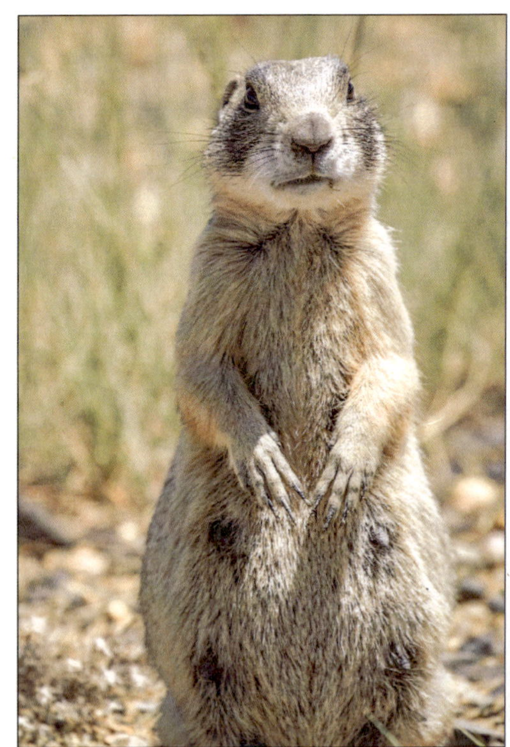

In 1979, black-footed ferrets were believed to be extinct, like the dinosaurs!

By killing (typically by poison) the vast majority of prairie dogs, people also killed black-footed ferrets (who ate the poisoned prairie dogs), and they took away the ferrets' food. These actions, and diseases that people brought to North America from other continents (sylvatic plague and canine distemper), wiped out the ferrets almost everywhere.

We almost lost black-footed ferrets forever.

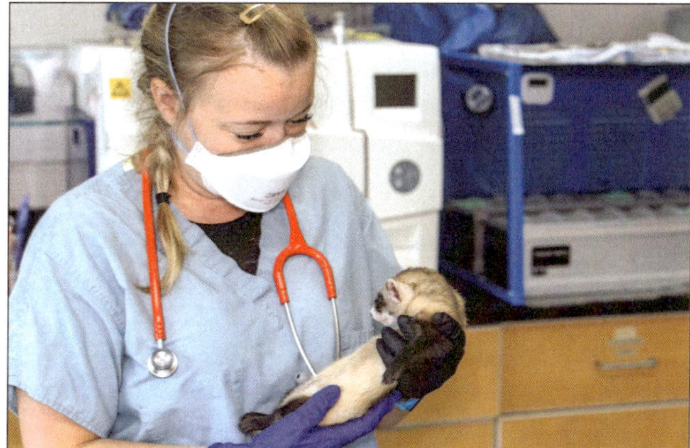

Wildlife veterinarian Dr. Stephanie Porter checks a ferret's body condition. Wildlife veterinarians help save black-footed ferrets by vaccinating them against diseases. They also give BFFs check-ups and microchips with unique identification numbers, so they can track how they are doing.

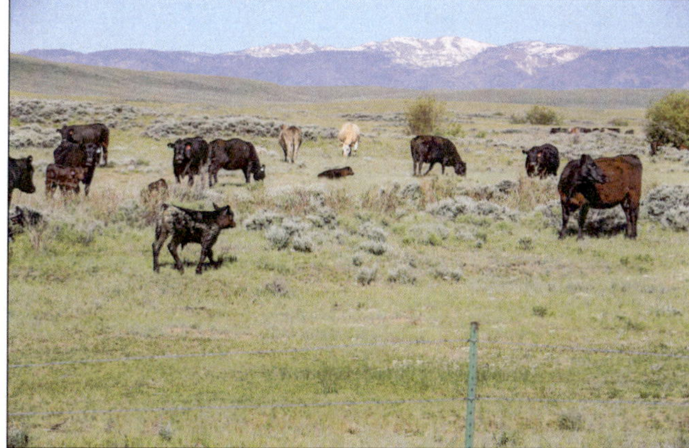

Prairie dogs and cattle can coexist. Prairie dogs do eat some of the grasses and other plants that cows eat. But prairie dogs only eat the tops of the grass (so they can see!), causing the grass roots to send more nutrients up into the shoots that cattle eat. When given a choice, cattle often prefer to graze on prairie dog towns, where the grass is more nutritious.

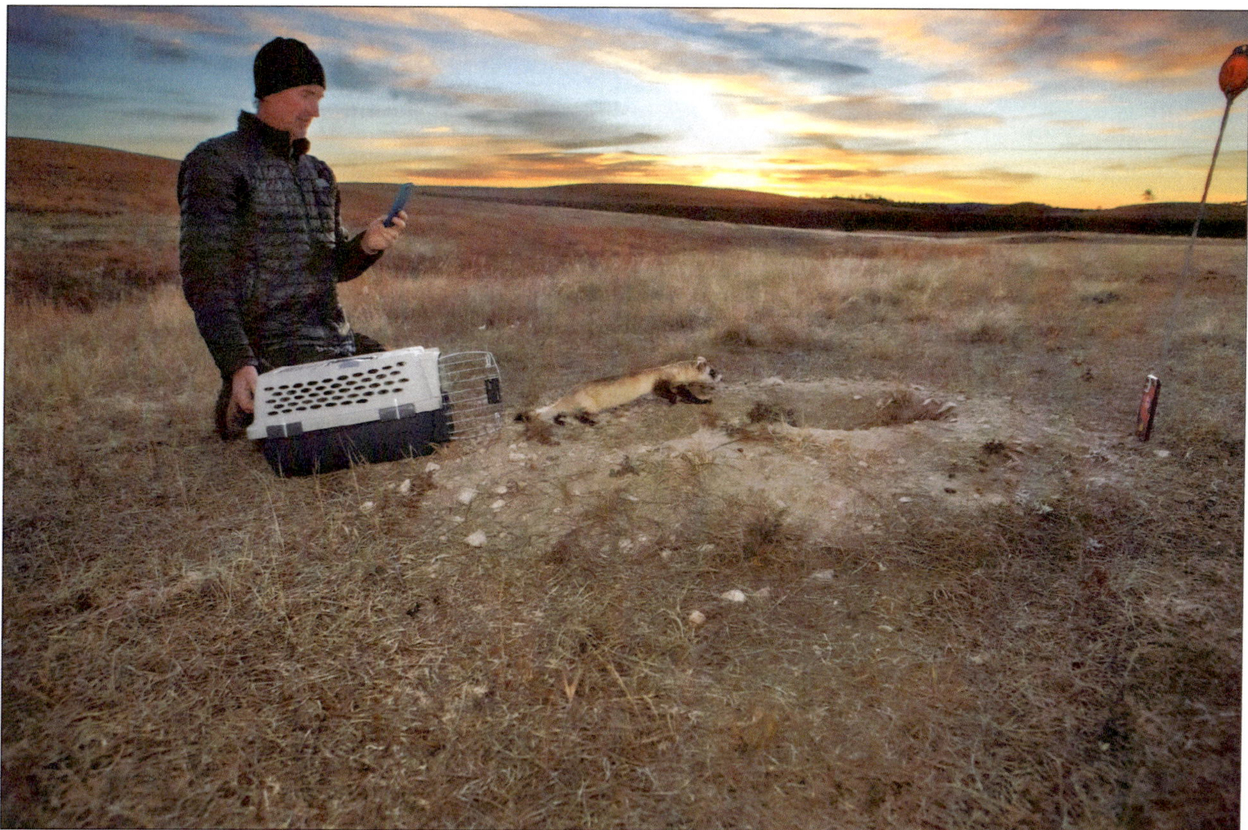

Freshly vaccinated and microchipped, each ferret returns to the same prairie dog hole.

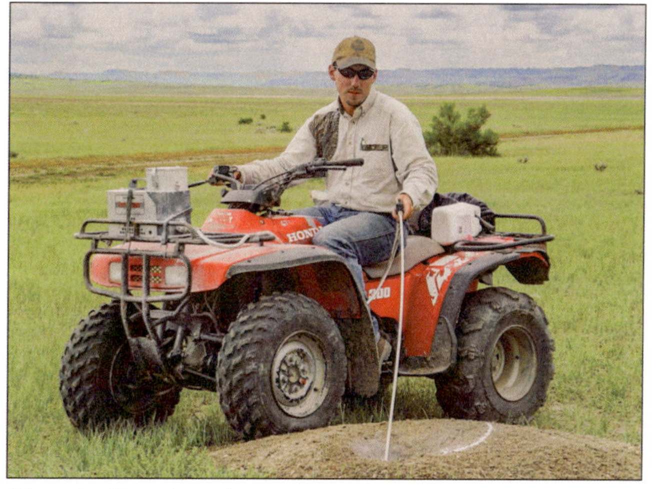

(Photo by Travis Livieri)

Plague can kill nearly all the black-footed ferrets and prairie dogs in an area. To help prevent plague outbreaks, biologists sprinkle thousands of prairie dog holes with a flea-killing dust. Unfortunately, dusting cannot always be performed due to cost and the time involved. A new anti-flea peanut-butter "treat" for prairie dogs holds some promise for keeping ferrets and prairie dogs healthy.

A Second Chance to Save Black-Footed Ferrets

Then, in 1981, a small population of black-footed ferrets was found in a prairie dog colony in Meeteetse, Wyoming. They were the last known black-footed ferrets on Earth.

But soon, diseases (both sylvatic plague and canine distemper) struck, and the Meeteetse ferrets were dying out. By winter of 1985-86, **only ten black-footed ferrets remained in the world.**

Six of the last ten ferrets were safe; they had already been brought into captivity for a breeding program. Four ferrets, including two females and a male known as "Scarface," were the only ferrets left in the wild. They needed to be rescued.

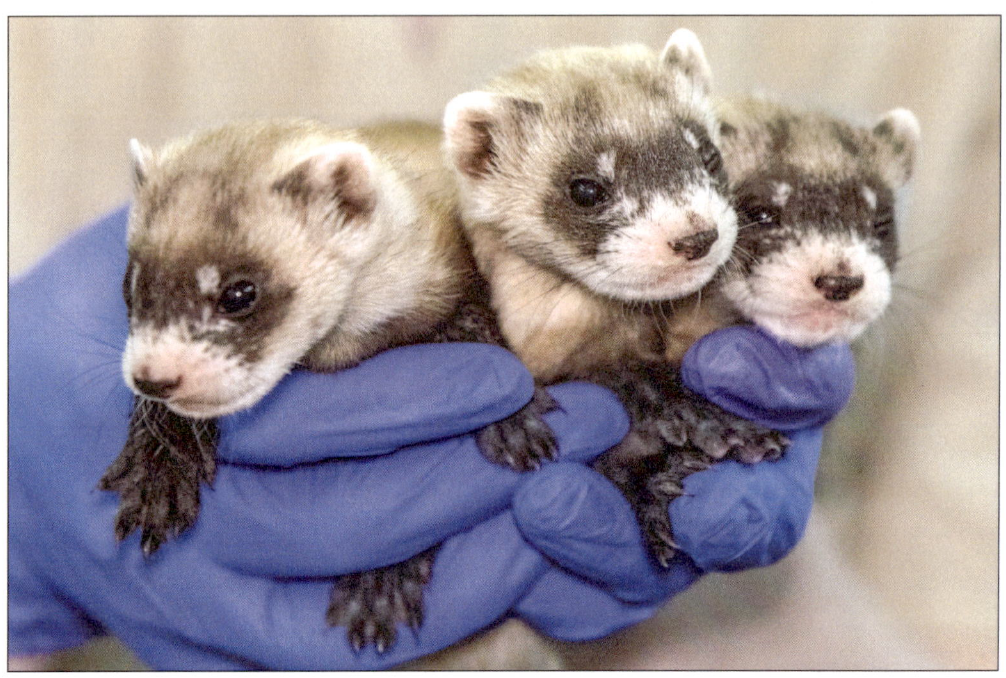

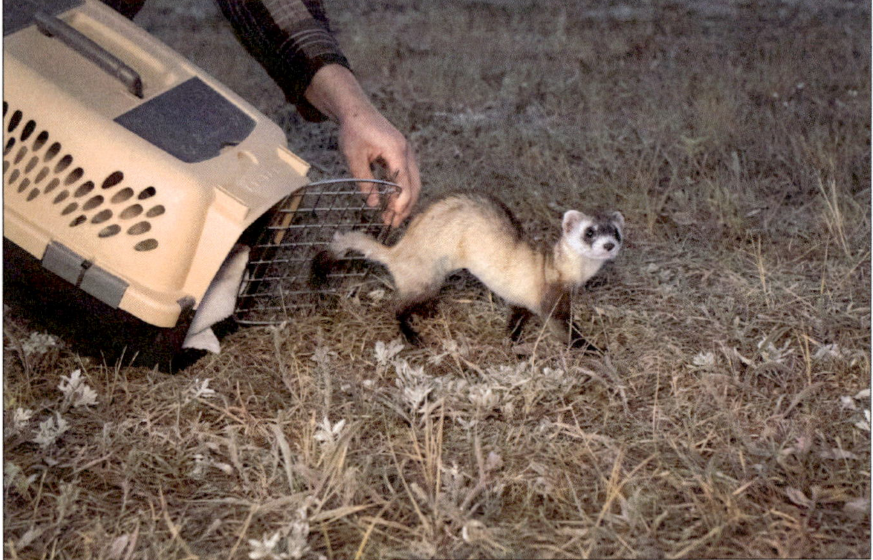

Every black-footed ferret living today is a descendant from a tiny family tree of just seven individual ferrets, known as founders, who successfully bred in the captive-breeding program.

Over time, biologists captured almost every wild ferret, including kits whom the two females gave birth to (which brought the total BFF population to eighteen). But they could not catch Scarface. A year went by, and no new kits were born.

Thankfully, biologists refused to give up, because once caught, Scarface went on to father several healthy, precious kits in captivity. Without Scarface, the captive-breeding program may not have succeeded. And by 1991, enough black-footed ferrets existed in the world that some could be released back to the wild.

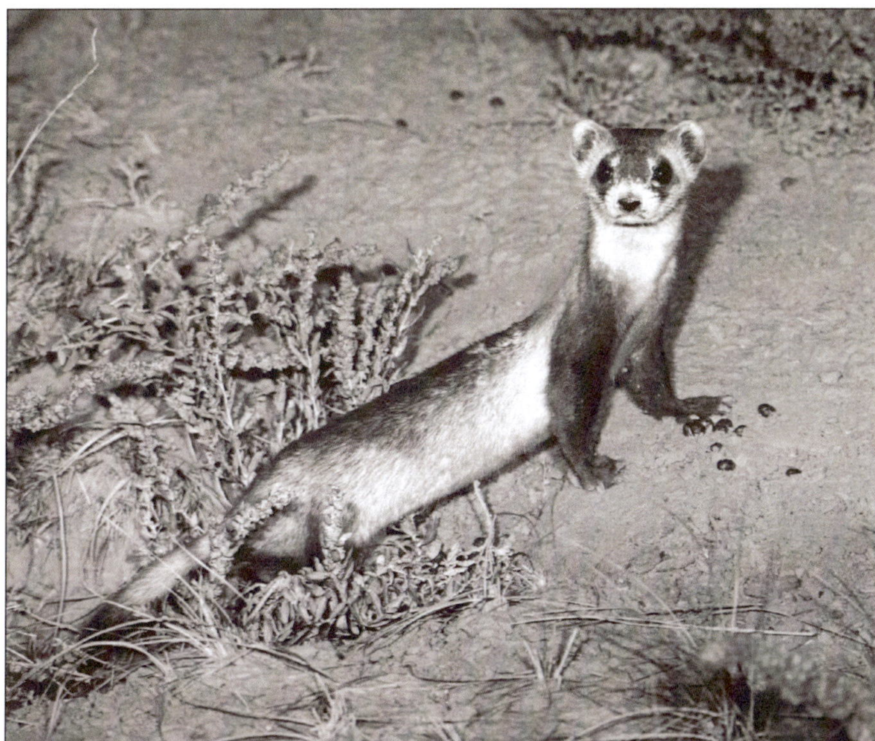

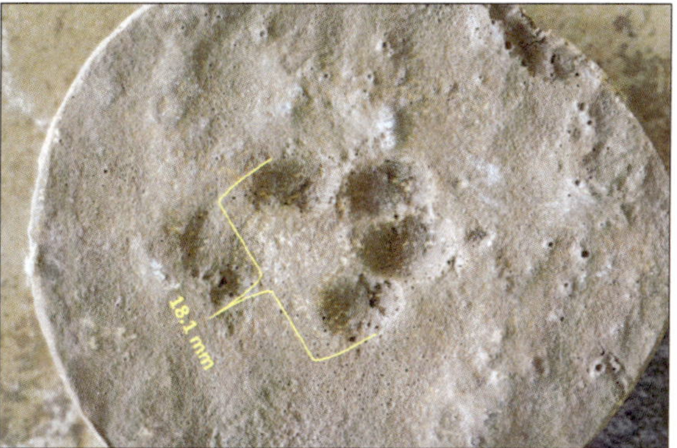

Mom's pawprint, actual size
(*Photo by Dr. Dean Biggins*)

This is "Mom," one of the original seven founders of the black-footed ferret captive-breeding program. She gave birth to twenty-one kits in captivity, and some of her kits had kits. She helped make the ferrets' return to the wild possible. (*Photo by Dr. Dean Biggins*)

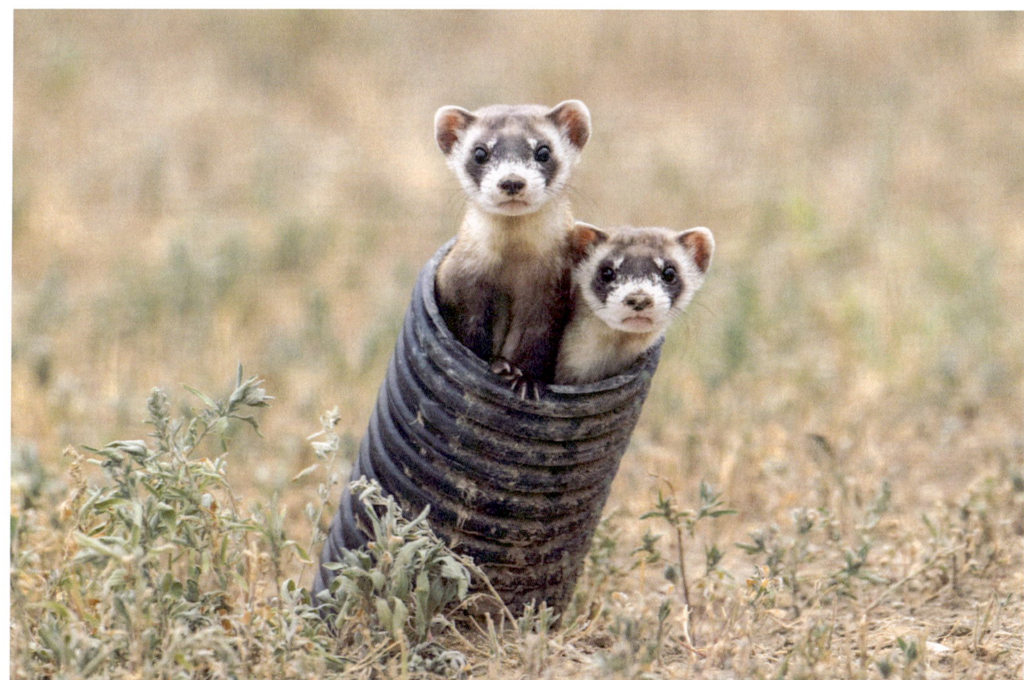

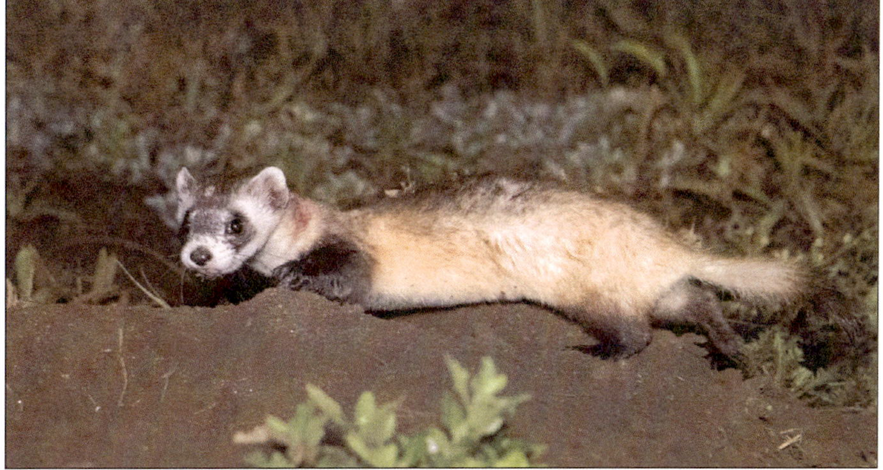

Black-footed ferrets typically do not live more than three years in nature.

During the early years, most captive-born ferrets released into the wild were killed by predators. Now, prior to release, ferret kits live in outdoor pens with underground tubes, like prairie dog burrows, for a month or longer to help them get used to hiding in nature. Scientists call this "preconditioning," and it has helped ferrets survive their first year in the wild by tenfold.

What Is an Endangered Species?

An endangered species, like the black-footed ferret, is at serious risk of going extinct and dying out from the Earth forever. Nothing will bring them back. The United States Endangered Species Act is the federal law that protects them.

"Black-footed ferrets live and die under the stars; they hunt and are hunted on the landscape. But it's what people do every day that keeps them from the brink of extinction."

—Kimberly Fraser
USFWS National Black-Footed Ferret Conservation Center

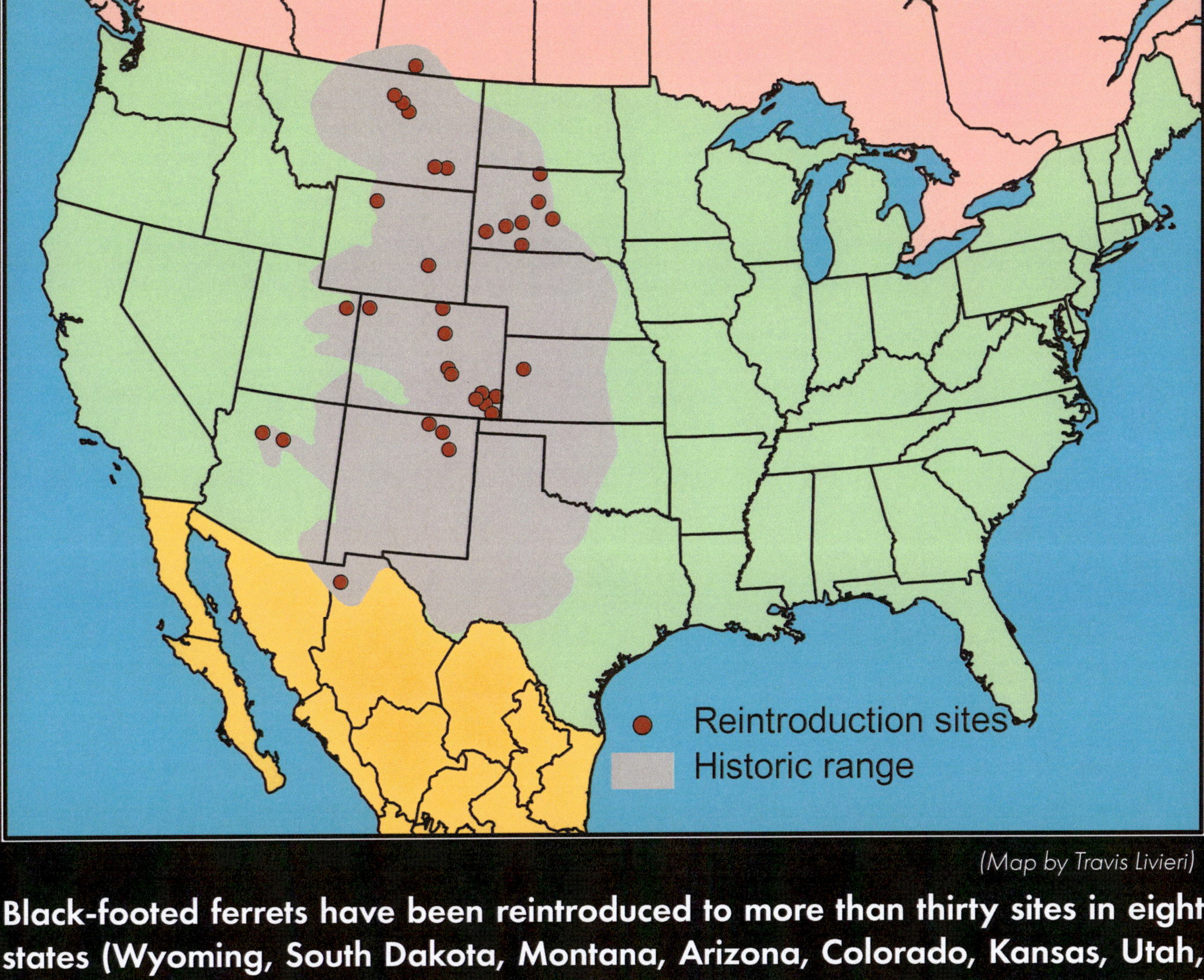

(Map by Travis Livieri)

Black-footed ferrets have been reintroduced to more than thirty sites in eight states (Wyoming, South Dakota, Montana, Arizona, Colorado, Kansas, Utah, and New Mexico), and in Canada, Mexico, and on Native American tribal lands. In some of these sites, ferrets are hanging on; in others, they have likely died out.

More prairie dog restoration and disease prevention are desperately needed.

By Saving Black-Footed Ferrets and Prairie Dogs, We Preserve an Ecosystem and More Than 130 Species of Prairie Animals and Plants

American bison (above) and pronghorns prefer to feed and spend their time among prairie dog colonies.

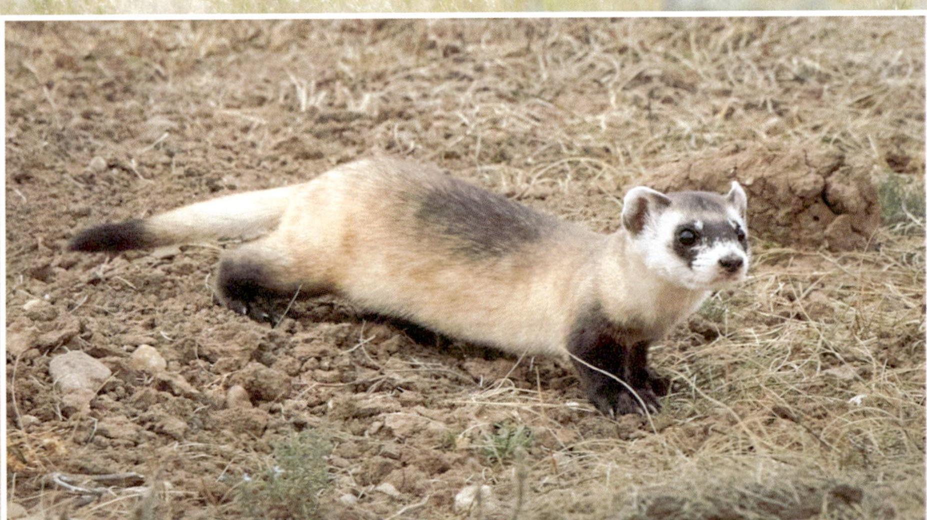

Black-footed ferrets are a flagship species of the prairie.

Prairie dogs are ecosystem engineers! Their digging mixes the soil, and their burrows provide homes for BFFs and other animals.

On the next page, check out more prairie animals.

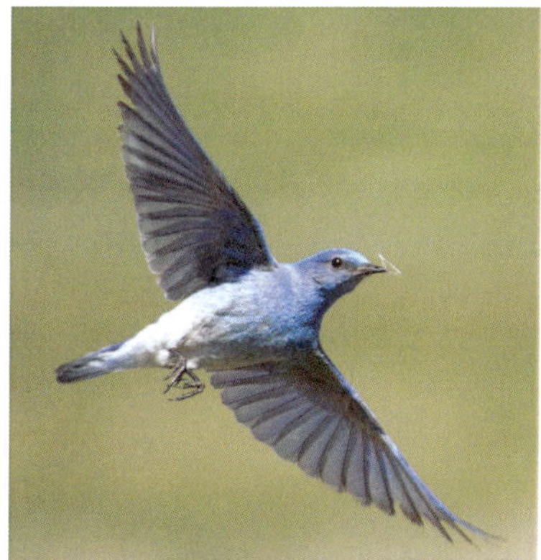

Mountain bluebird

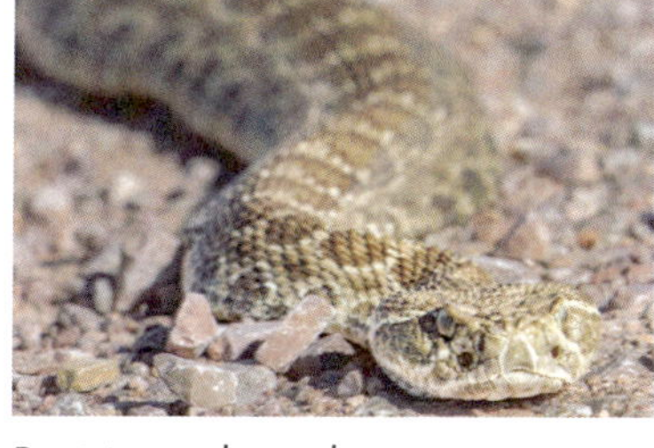

Prairie rattlesnake

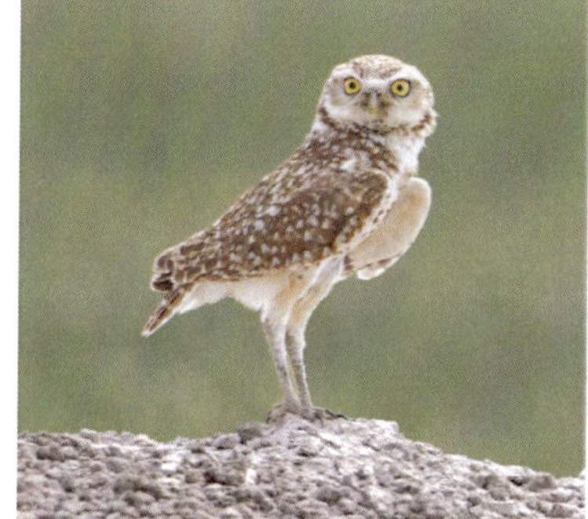

Burrowing owls lay their eggs and raise their young in prairie dog holes.

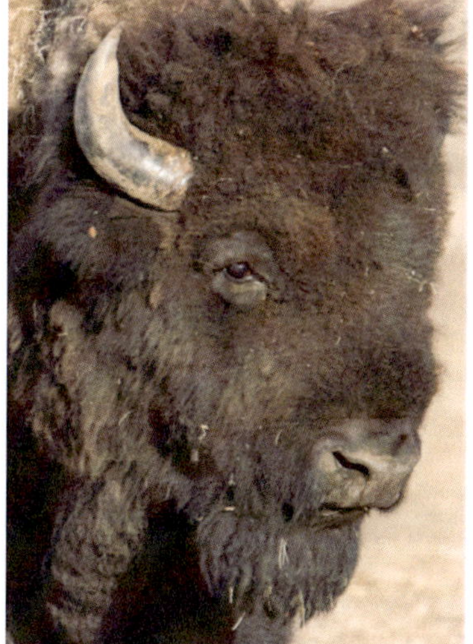

American bison

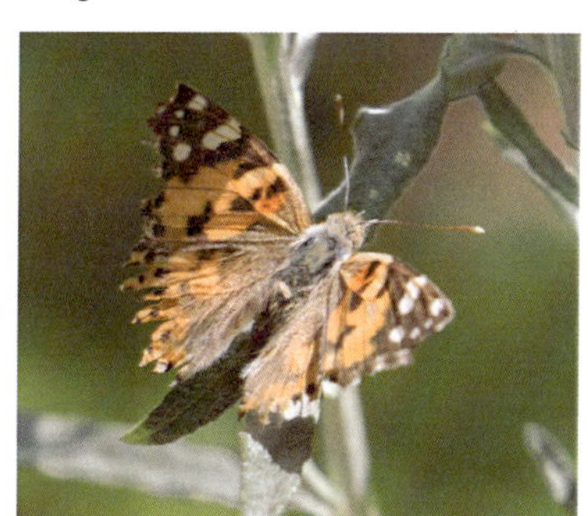

Painted lady

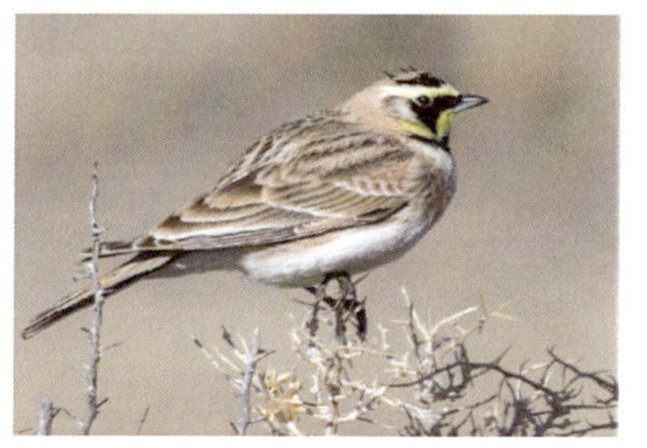

Horned lark

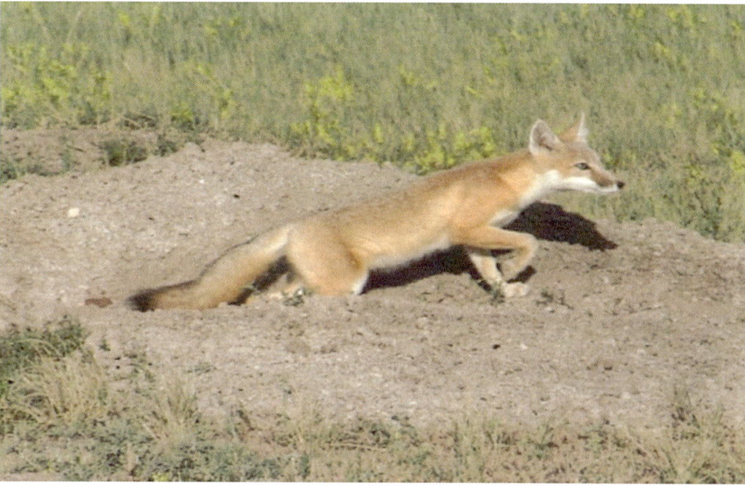

Swift fox *(Photo by Travis Livieri)*

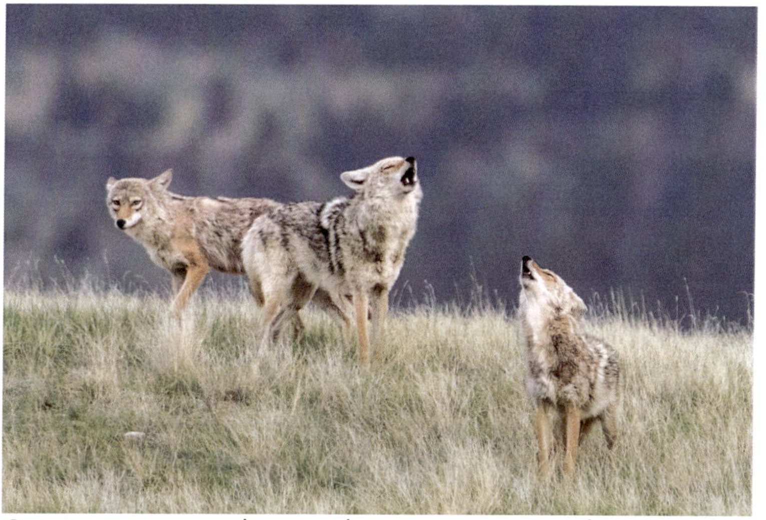

Coyotes are among the more than twenty species of predator that hunt prairie dogs for food.

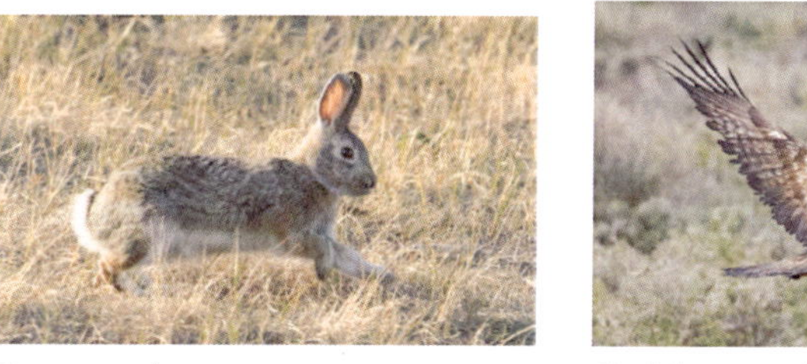

Cottontail

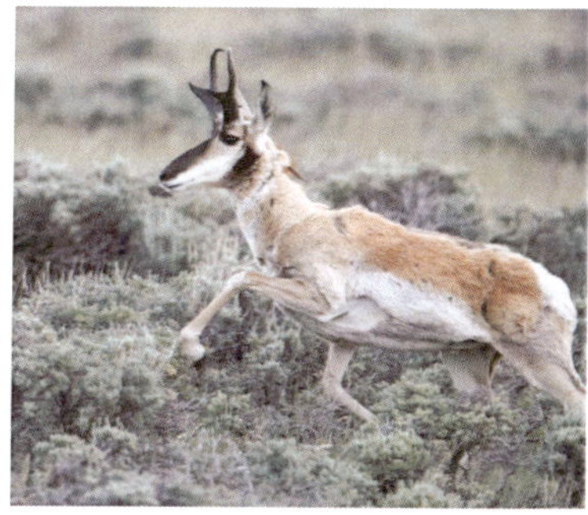

Pronghorn

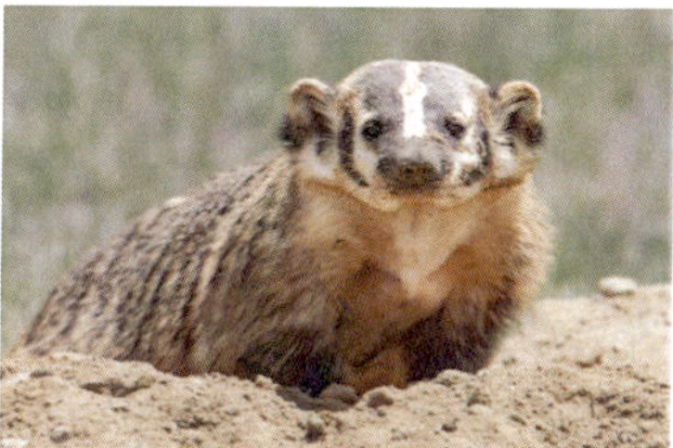

American badger

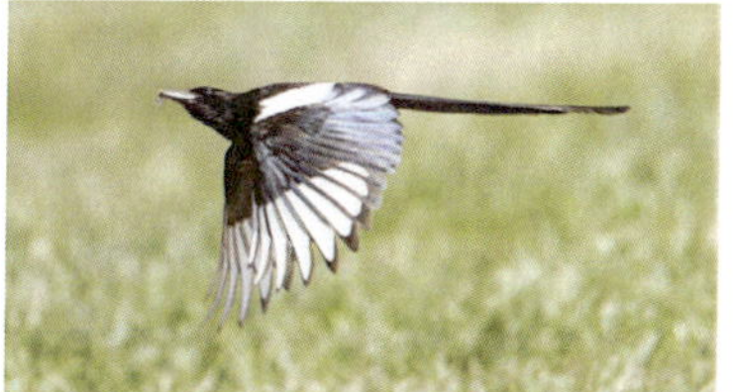

Black-billed magpie

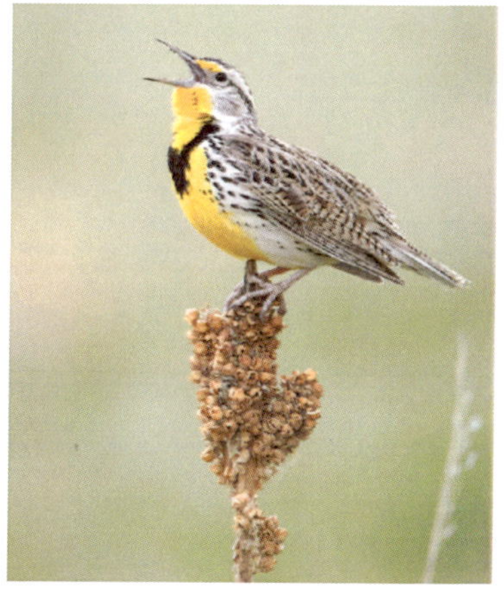

Western meadowlark

Western tiger salamander
(Courtesy of the National Park Service)

Golden eagle

How You Can Help Black-Footed Ferrets

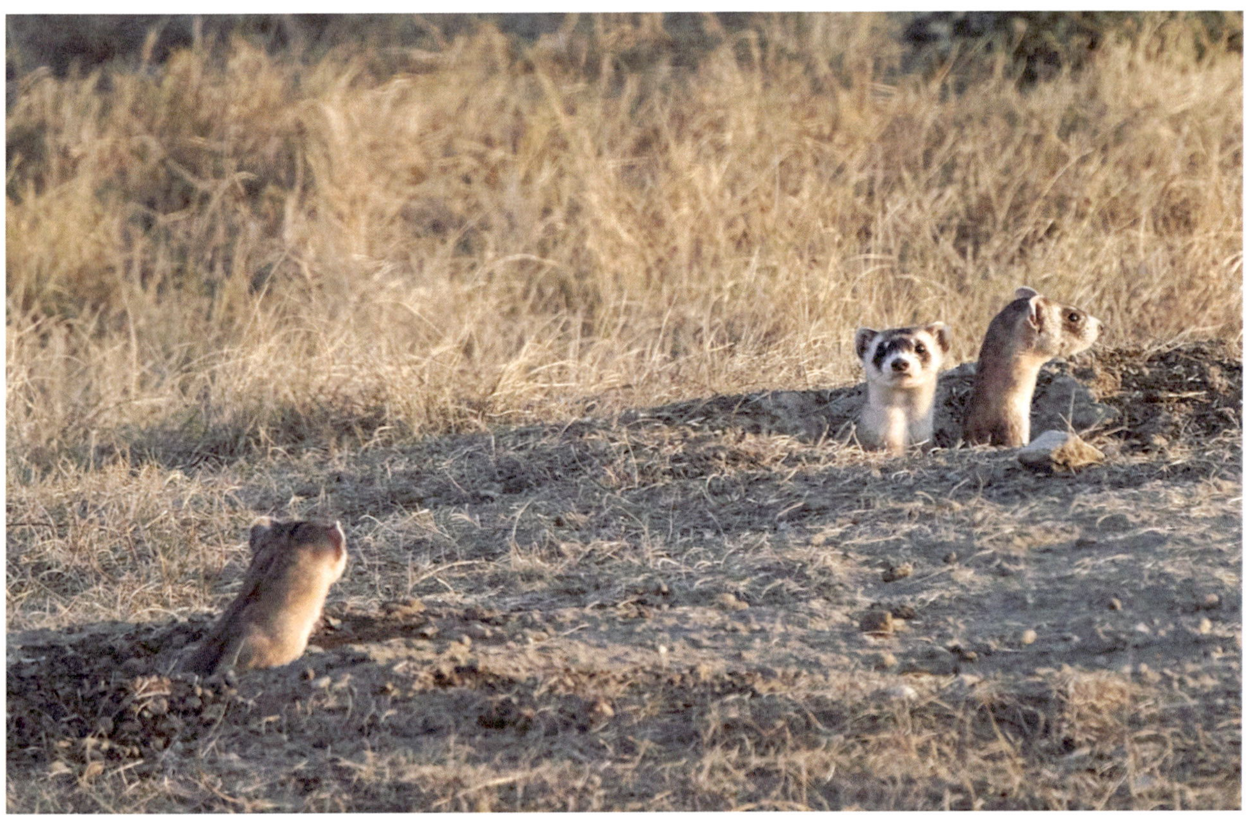

- **Share the care** for endangered black-footed ferrets with family, friends, teachers, and others in your community.

- **Support zoos that support ferret recovery,** such as the Louisville Zoo, Phoenix Zoo, Cheyenne Mountain Zoo, Toronto Zoo, and Smithsonian Conservation Biology Institute. Additional refuges, museums, and discovery centers have ferrets on display.

- **Experience the joys of prairie dogs** at a national park, wildlife refuge, zoo, or other habitat with prairie dog towns.

- **Explore the prairie** and see some of the **more than 130 species** we save when we save black-footed ferrets.

Ferret-Conservation Organizations

BlackFootedFerret.org
www.blackfootedferret.org

Prairie Wildlife Research
prairiewildlife.org

Defenders of Wildlife
defenders.org/wildlife/black-footed-ferret

World Wildlife Fund
www.worldwildlife.org/species/black-footed-ferret

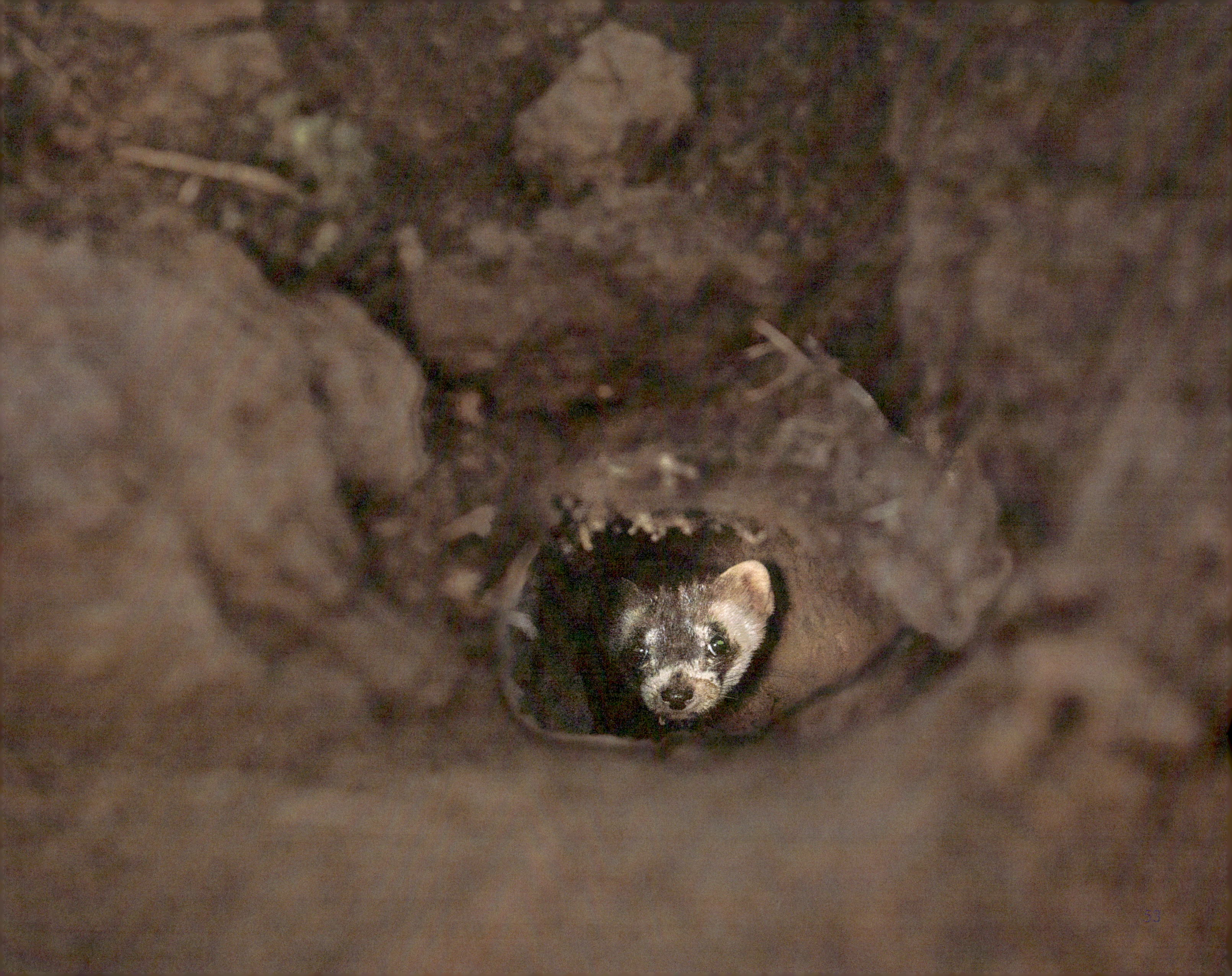

Ferret Resources

For kids!

Black-Footed Ferrets: Back from the Brink by Miriam Aronin (Bearport Publishing, 2008).

Bringing Back the Black-Footed Ferret by Rachel Stuckey (Crabtree Publishing Company, 2020).

For all!

Prairie Night: Black-Footed Ferrets and the Recovery of an Endangered Species by Brian Miller, Richard P. Reading, and Steve Forrest (The Smithsonian Institution, 1996).

Wild Again: The Struggle to Save the Black-Footed Ferret by David Jachowski (University of California Press, 2014).

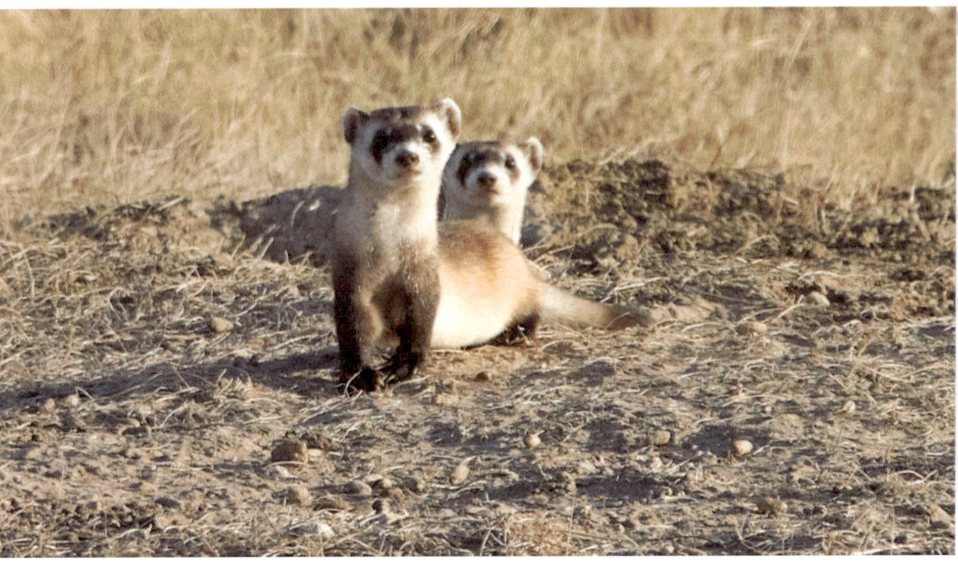

Videos:

 Black-Footed Ferrets (National Geographic): https://www.youtube.com/watch?v=7IOXtYmtRG8

 Black-Footed Ferrets: The Rediscovery (Wyoming Game and Fish Department): https://www.youtube.com/watch?v=1U-YCXjf4_I

 Dodging Extinction: The Black-Footed Ferret Recovery Program (US Fish & Wildlife Service): https://www.youtube.com/watch?v=YbwqDBC7Bu4

 Ferret Town (Caldera Productions): https://calderaproductions.com/ferret-town/

 How the Black-Footed Ferret Is Making a Comeback from the Brink of Extinction (PBS NewsHour): https://www.youtube.com/watch?v=GAvYWXDyY3s

 WILD HOPE: The Decades-Long Fight to Save America's Black-Footed Ferret (Nature on PBS): https://www.youtube.com/watch?v=Ll3HRgnBd5gvv

Websites:

 Mutual of Omaha's Wild Kingdom: Return of the Black-Footed Ferret: https://www.mutualofomaha.com/wild-kingdom/article/return-of-the-black-footed-ferret

 *National Park Service: Black-Footed Ferret: Rebounding in the Badlands*: https://www.nps.gov/articles/000/black-footed-ferret-badl.htm

 National Park Service: Masked Bandits: Black-Footed Ferrets in Wind Cave: https://www.nps.gov/articles/000/black-footed-ferret-wica.htm

 Smithsonian's National Zoo & Conservation Biology Institute: Black-Footed Ferret: https://nationalzoo.si.edu/animals/black-footed-ferret

 The Nature Conservancy: Animals We Protect: Black-Footed Ferret: https://www.nature.org/en-us/get-involved/how-to-help/animals-we-protect/black-footed-ferret/

 US Fish & Wildlife Service: Black-Footed Ferret: https://www.fws.gov/species/black-footed-ferret-mustela-nigripes

Prairie Dog Resources

For kids!

Prairie Dogs (Our Wild World) by Marybeth Lorbiecki (Cooper Square Publishing, 2004).

For all!

Conservation of the Black-Tailed Prairie Dog: Saving North America's Western Grasslands edited by John L. Hoogland (Island Press, 2005).

Prairie Dogs: Ecology and Social Behavior by John L. Hoogland (Princeton University Press, projected for 2026).

 **Prairie Dog Coalition**
https://www.prairiedogcoalition.org/

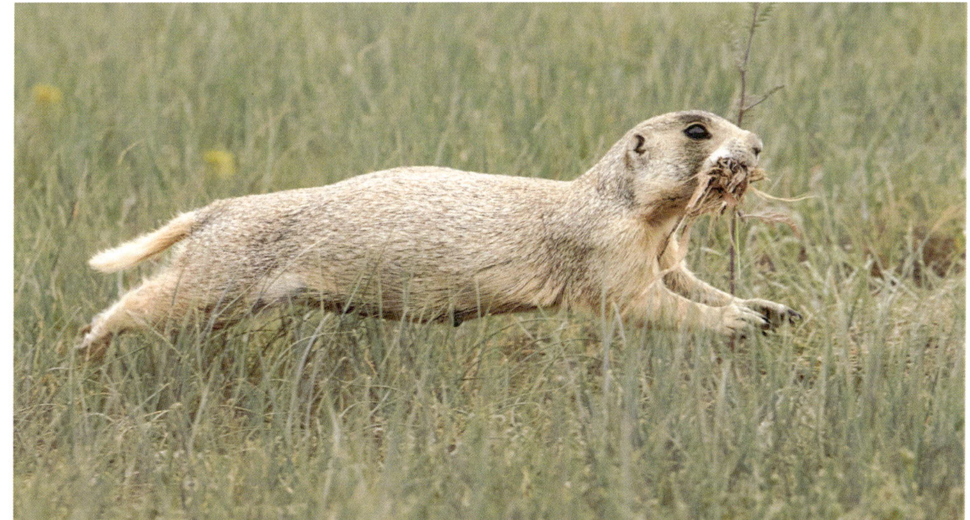

Prairie dog with nesting material.

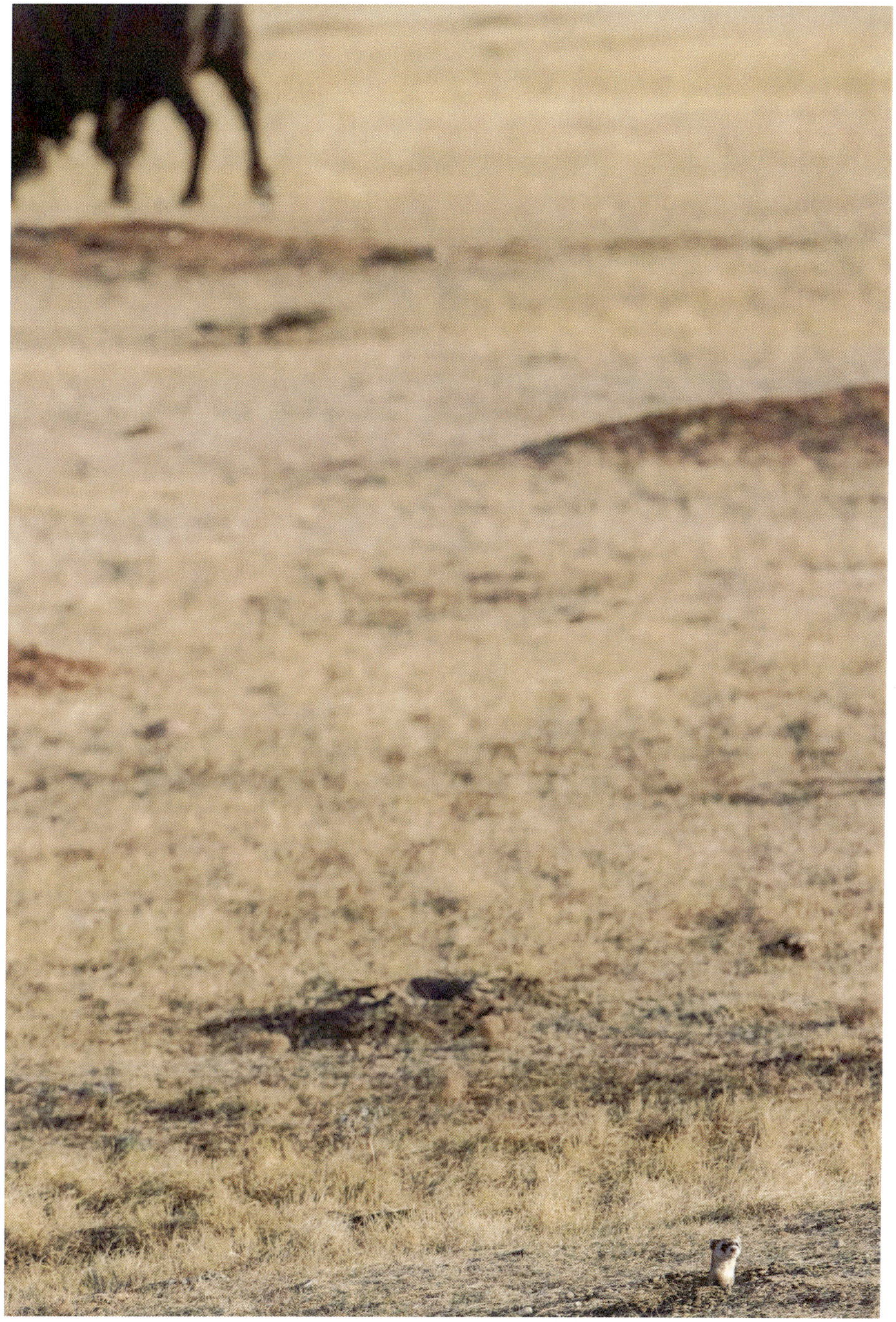

Black-footed ferret with an American bison on the prairie.

An Interview with Dr. Dean Biggins

As a biologist, Dr. Dean Biggins (US Geological Survey) has dedicated forty-four years to black-footed ferret conservation. He and his field team captured twelve of the eighteen ferrets that formed the captive breeding program. All of these ferrets "were individuals with a story," says Dean, especially Mom and Scarface, the most successful breeders in the program. Dean's valuable contributions to science have helped keep black-footed ferrets in existence, and not extinction, and slinking and scampering about our world today.

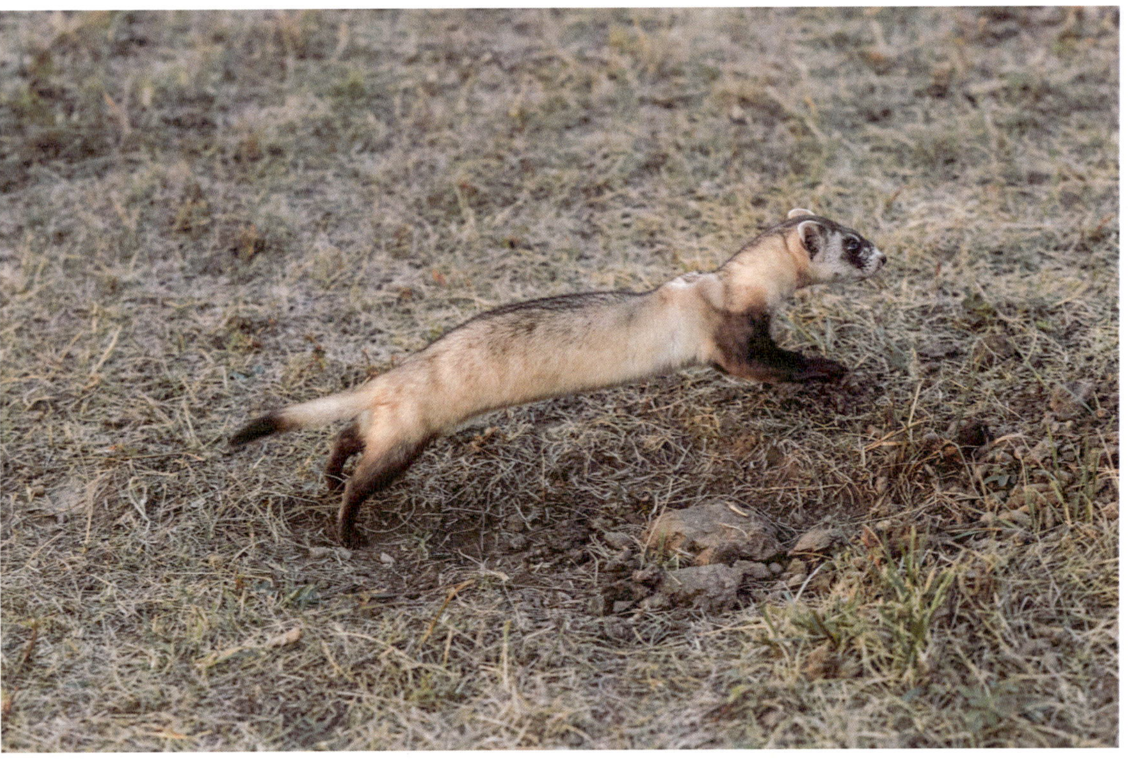

Elaine Miller Bond:
Twice during the 1900s, black-footed ferrets were believed to be extinct. How did you feel when a small ferret population was rediscovered in 1981?

Dr. Dean Biggins:
Elation best describes the overall feeling of all three of my colleagues and I who arrived on the scene after Shep, John Hogg's dog, discovered the ferret near Meeteetse, Wyoming. My first sighting of a ferret, a few days later, was awe-inspiring. We spent endless hours working with the ferrets, with only obligatory bouts of sleeping and eating.

There was also a bit of apprehension—any mistakes could have dire consequences. We were trying to figure out what to do with what we thought might well be the last individuals of a species.

Elaine:
What has motivated you for forty-four years, working to save black-footed ferrets?

Dean:
In the fifth grade, I got into trouble for designing a "coat-of-arms" with my initials and a big, green letter "N" for Nature, instead of doing my assigned class work. Even at that early age, I felt an affinity

and reverence for the natural world and believed something needed to be done about the human abuses of nature. My shield implied a battle ahead.

Another tendency is my stubbornness, which became an asset in not giving up when the odds seemed to be against us. There were cycles of immense frustration and disappointment. Yet the successes were inspirational and gave me hope, for example, the sudden upswing in captive-bred ferrets in 1986 after Scarface was captured, the improvements in post-release ferret survival due to pen-rearing (preconditioning), the re-establishment of free-ranging ferrets in the wild, and the development of methods to manage plague (a non-native disease and the biological nemesis to ferret recovery). All told, there was no way I could consider giving up.

Elaine:
What lessons have black-footed ferrets taught you?

Dean:
First, think ahead—when a species is in peril, try to determine why and start proactive conservation measures immediately. Second, science is critically important. Controlled experiments that help determine why the species is in jeopardy give more reliable results than "just trying something."

Elaine:
Why is it important to save black-footed ferrets?

Dean:
Each species is part of a much larger ecosystem, and losing a species causes changes in the entire system. Some of those changes are obvious. But we humans are probably incapable of detecting many of them. We need to be humble about what we think we know.

I think all life on Earth has value. It goes beyond the values we humans normally relate to, such as money or the value (if any) a living being provides to humans or other species. Environmental ethics philosophers call this "intrinsic value." We must conserve black-footed ferrets, simply because they are living beings, for their own sake.

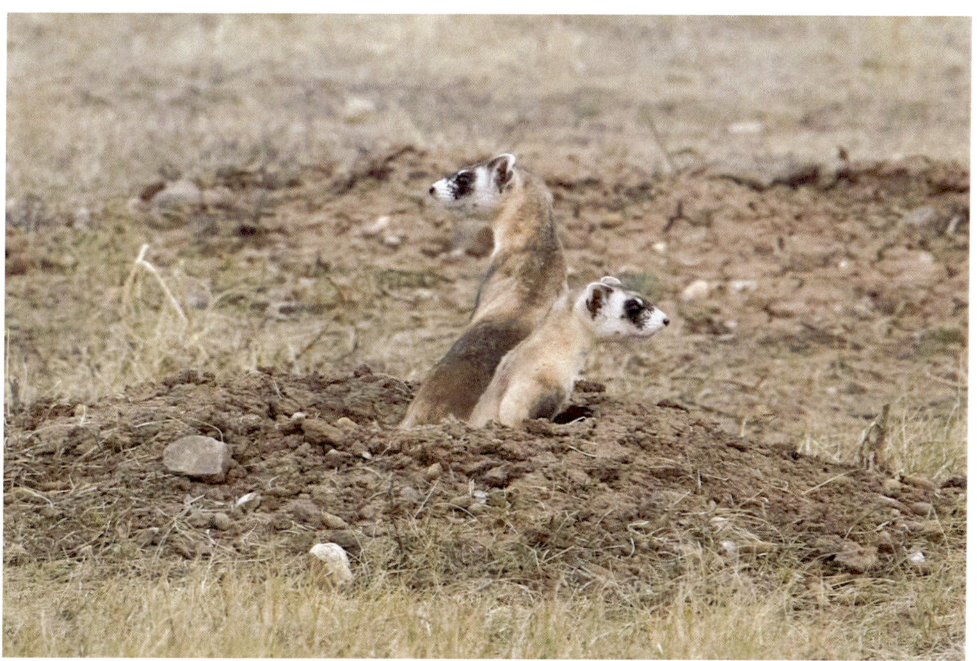

For the black-footed ferrets and their human friends working to save them

Thank you to the experts who graciously helped with this book: Angela R. Jarding (National Park Service), Dr. Dean Biggins (US Geological Survey), Dr. Travis Livieri (Prairie Wildlife Research), Dr. John L. Hoogland (University of Maryland at Frostburg), Tina S. Jackson, Justin Chuven, and Kimberly Fraser (three experts from the US Fish and Wildlife Service (USFWS) National Black-Footed Ferret Conservation Center), Sarah Metzer (USFWS), Dr. Stephanie Porter (USFWS), Dr. Richard P. Reading (Butterfly Pavilion), and Dr. David S. Jachowski (Clemson University). And heartfelt thanks to: Terry Tempest Williams, Gail Hochman, Marc Ohms, Aaren Nellen, Angela Garvey, the Village Books Picture Book Critique Group, Dr. Kris Johnson, Natalie McDougall, Connie Miller, the Miller Family, M.J. Bogatin, and my wondrous editors, E. Janae Byrd, Susan Gee Rumsey, and Molly Woodward. Words cannot fully express my gratitude to Kate Jordahl and Geir Jordahl, True North Editions, for publishing this dream of a book.

My gratitude also extends to the fifty different partners—state and federal agencies, zoos, nonprofit organizations, Native American tribes, and private land owners—on the frontlines of black-footed ferret conservation.

The photographs in this book of black-footed ferrets and other wildlife were created in many locations in North America. I am indebted to people, past and present, particularly Indigenous peoples and cultures, for their care of the black-footed ferrets. I also thank them for their generosity and welcoming spirit over the years of this project. Black-footed ferrets have been welcomed back to Native American tribal lands more than any other kind of land. Thank you to all the people who work to preserve the land and the lives of this amazing and important animal.

Photographs in this book depict wild black-footed ferrets and other animals in their natural habitats, except for the captive-born ferret kits on pages 24, 25, 45, 46, and 47. Photographs were captured on a camera and document real moments as they happened.

Elaine Miller Bond made all images except as noted.
- page 24 by Kimberly Fraser
- pages 45, 49, 51 by Travis Livieri
- page 47 by Dr. Dean Biggins
- page 51 courtesy of the National Park Service

Warm thanks to all contributors.

Elaine Miller Bond loves writing and taking photographs, especially for young people, because they care about saving precious living things, like black-footed ferrets. For her other books and more: www.elainemillerbond.com.

A Note from the Author/Photographer

To be a wildlife photographer, one needs a love and respect for animals, strong muscles (cameras with long lenses are heavy!), and most of all, patience. In fact, I waited eighteen years before I ever got to see an endangered black-footed ferret.

My adventures in photography began in 2004, when I took pictures of prairie dogs and their fun behaviors with a professor who studies them. Over the years, I returned to my beloved prairie and prairie dogs in Utah, South Dakota, Colorado, Wyoming, and New Mexico. Always I dreamed of seeing a black-footed ferret. But I never expected my dream to come true, because black-footed ferrets are so rare and endangered—and once thought to be extinct—in addition to their secretive lifestyle. And when I was starting out, black-footed ferrets had only been reintroduced to a few locations. So I cried happy tears in the middle of one cold, windy night in South Dakota, when I saw my first precious black-footed ferret, my dream ferret. She is the beautiful four-and-a-half-month-old kit on page 26. She, like every living black-footed ferret, represents resilience, second chances, and the kind of wild hope that slinks, prowls, and dances on the prairie on little furry black feet.

—*Elaine Miller Bond*

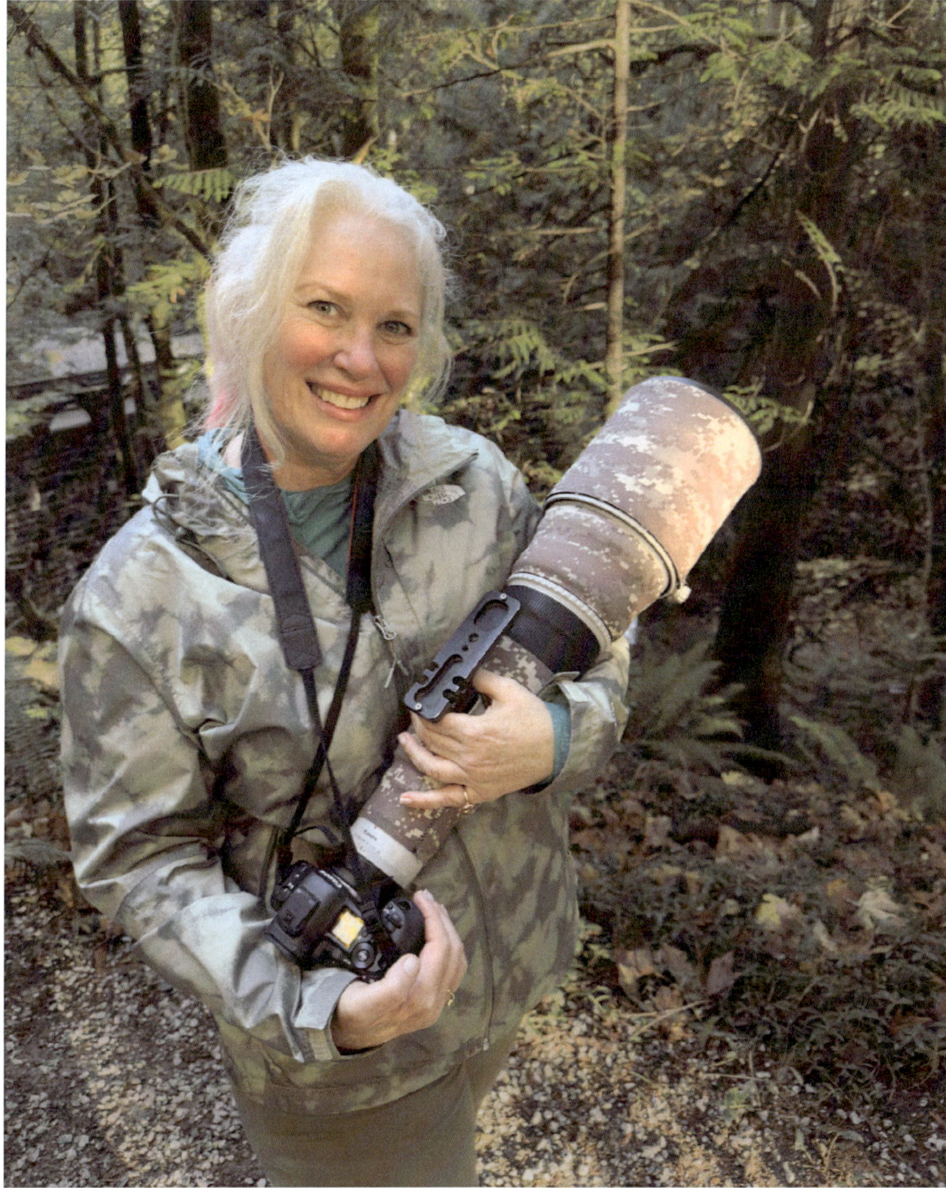

Elaine with her wildlife photography kit: a 500mm fixed lens with a 1.4x teleconverter (which gives the lens a 700mm reach) on a full-frame Canon camera. Like a telescope, the long telephoto lens helps the photographer keep their distance from the animals, and the animals act naturally. Most importantly, the photographer shows maximum respect to the wildlife, and everyone stays safe. *(Photo by E. Janae Byrd)*

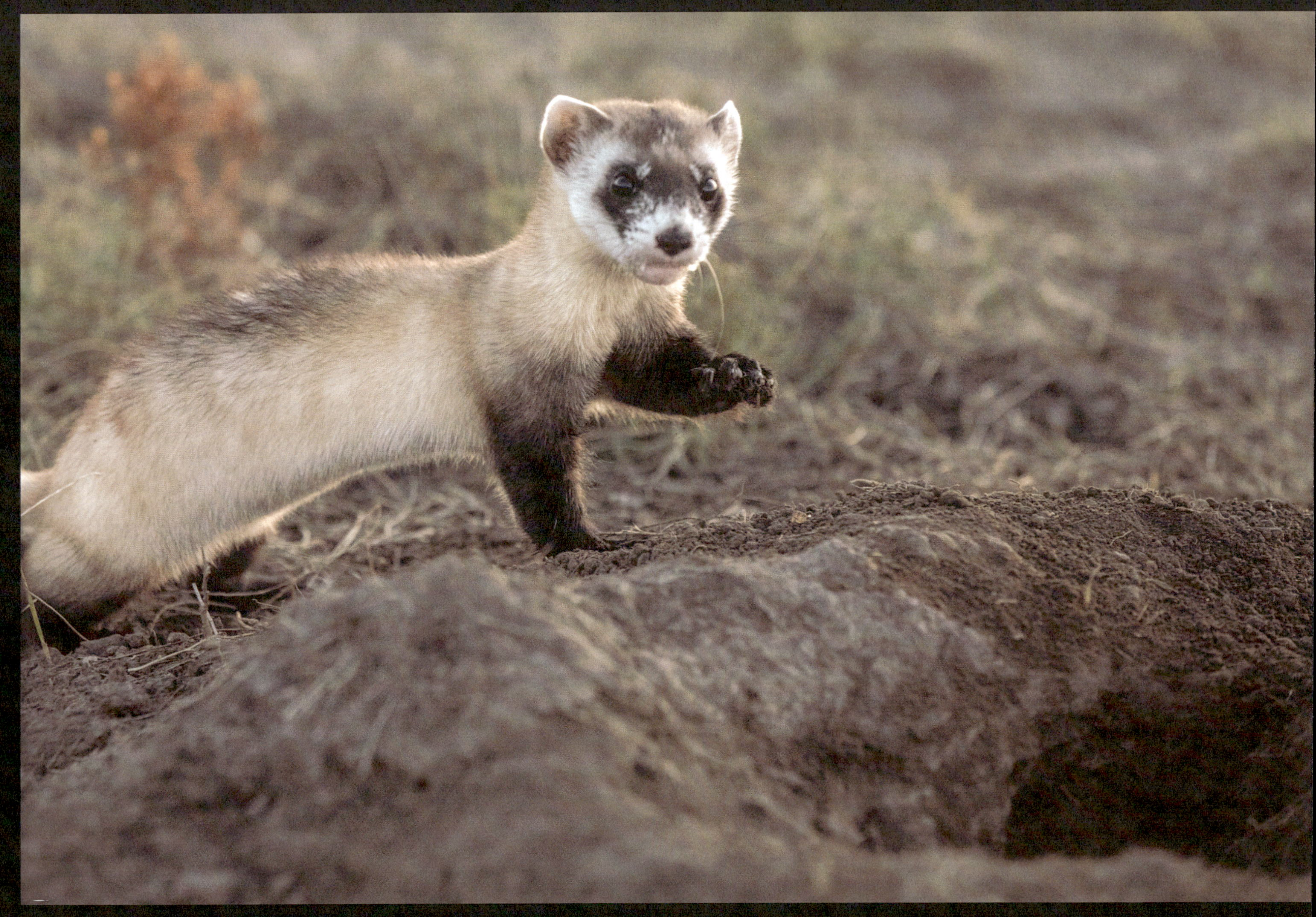

At THE END of a busy night. . .

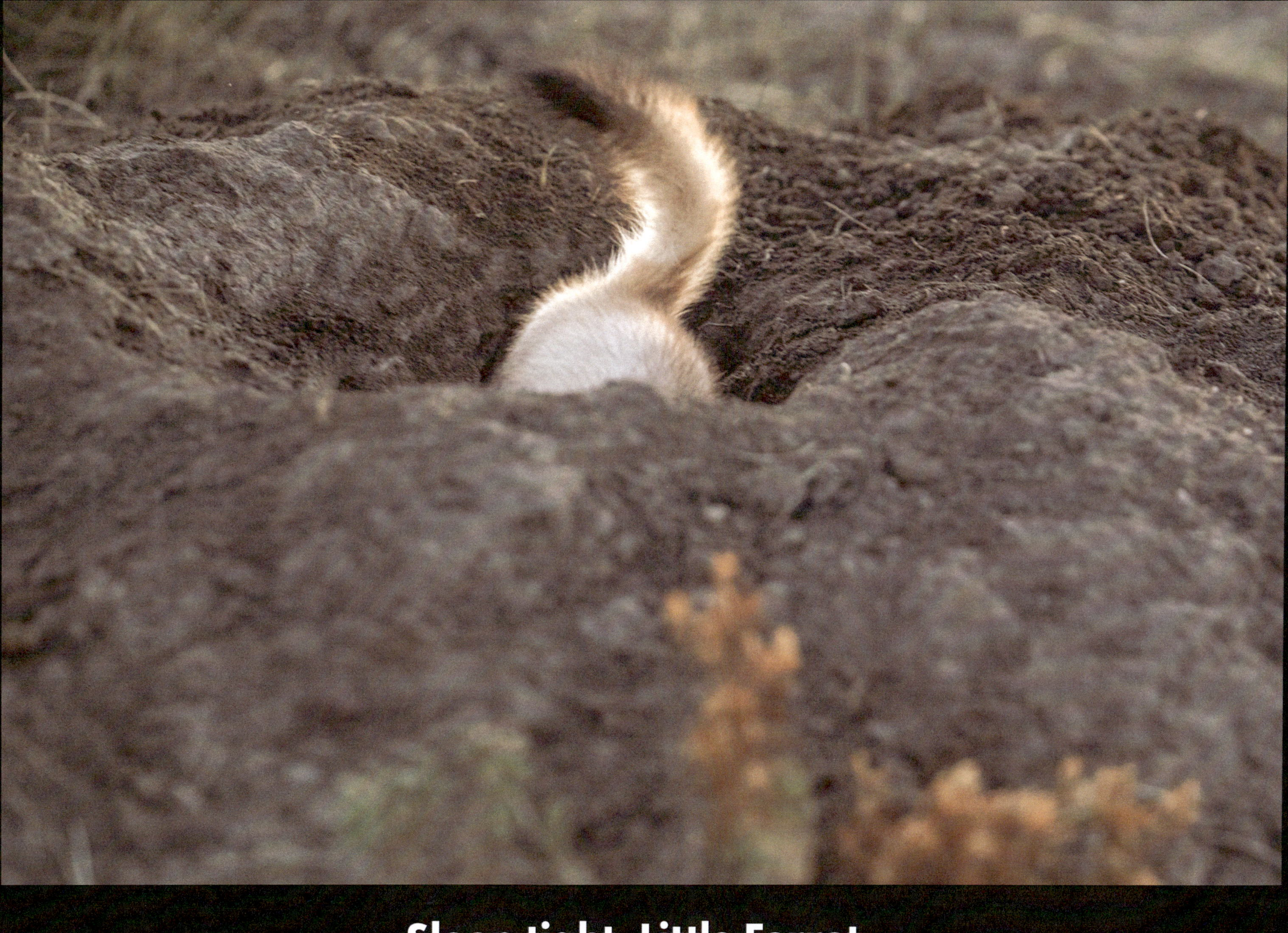

Sleep tight, Little Ferret.